RAIMUND ABRAHAM & THE AUSTRIAN CULTURAL FORUM NEW YORK

RAIMUND ABRAHAM & THE AUSTRIAN CULTURAL FORUM NEW YORK

Herausgegeben von | Edited by
Andres Lepik und | and
Andreas Stadler

Mit Beiträgen von |
With essays by
Peter Engelmann
Kenneth Frampton
Andres Lepik
Peter Marboe
Gerald Matt
Andreas Stadler
Lebbeus Woods

Mit Fotografien von |
With photographs by
David Plakke und | and
Robert Polidori

Andres Lepik, Andreas Stadler
VORWORT 8
FOREWORD 12

Andreas Stadler
DAS ÖSTERREICHISCHE KULTURFORUM NEW YORK: LEUCHTTURM UND TRÄGERRAKETE 16
THE AUSTRIAN CULTURAL FORUM NEW YORK: LIGHTHOUSE AND CARRIER ROCKET 30

Andres Lepik
GEGEN DEN STROM 46
AGAINST THE TIDE 56

RAIMUND ABRAHAM IM GESPRÄCH MIT Gerald Matt 64
RAIMUND ABRAHAM IN CONVERSATION WITH Gerald Matt 72

Peter Engelmann
RAIMUND ABRAHAM: EIN POSTMODERNER DENKER UND DEKONSTRUKTIVISTISCHER ARCHITEKT 82
RAIMUND ABRAHAM: A POSTMODERN THINKER AND DECONSTRUCTIVIST ARCHITECT 86

Lebbeus Woods
EIN HERAUSFORDERNDES VERMÄCHTNIS 90
A CHALLENGING LEGACY 100

KENNETH FRAMPTON IM GESPRÄCH MIT Andres Lepik und Andreas Stadler 104
KENNETH FRAMPTON IN CONVERSATION WITH Andres Lepik and Andreas Stadler 108

Peter Marboe
EIN TRAUM WIRD WAHR 114
A DREAM COME TRUE 118

Anhang 124
Appendix 126

Andres Lepik, Andreas Stadler

VORWORT

Als 1992 der in New York lebende und lehrende Raimund Abraham aus einem einzigartigen Wettbewerb zum Neubau des Österreichischen Kulturforums als Sieger hervorging, begann damit eine zwar schwierige, jedoch schlussendlich erfolgreiche Reise – sowohl für den Architekten als auch für die Republik Österreich als Bauherrin. Schon der Entschluss, den Wettbewerb für alle Architekten »österreichischer Herkunft« öffentlich auszuschreiben und die Entscheidung einer hochrangigen Jury mit internationaler Besetzung zu überlassen, galt als mutig und wurde vom Inspirator und Organisator Ernst Bliem ausführlich dokumentiert. Dass dieses – gemessen an den räumlichen Dimensionen Manhattans – verhältnismäßig kleine Projekt schon unmittelbar nach seiner Veröffentlichung bereits 1993 eine Ausstellung im Museum of Modern Art erhielt, wies auf die besondere Bedeutung hin, die ihm schon von Anfang an zugemessen wurde.

Sechs Jahre später, 1999, und nach einer Phase, in der das Projekt schon beinahe zu scheitern drohte, zeigte das Architekturzentrum Wien die Ausstellung *Manhattan, Austria. The Architecture of the Austrian Cultural Institute by Raimund Abraham* in der Ovalhalle des Wiener Museumsquartiers und publizierte dazu einen Katalog, der sowohl einen Überblick über die Institution, den Wettbewerb als auch die Detailplanung bot. Danach begann die Bauphase, die angesichts dieses komplexen Entwurfs erwartungsgemäß noch weitere Herausforderungen für alle Beteiligten brachte. Denn in New York ist das Baugewerbe nicht wirklich auf die hohe Qualität eingestellt, die hier verlangt wurde.

Doch die Anstrengungen, die von allen Seiten unternommen wurden, um diese einzigartige Architektur zu realisieren, haben sich ausgezahlt. Seit 2002, als das

Gebäude mit großer internationaler Aufmerksamkeit eröffnet wurde, ist das Kulturforum ein festes Ziel vieler architekturinteressierter Touristen geworden, und es bleibt weiterhin ein wichtiger Anlaufpunkt der architektonischen Fachwelt. Sowohl die Bewunderer des Designs des Hauses als auch die vielen Veranstaltungsbesucher haben immer wieder nach einer aktuellen Publikation zur Architektur, Funktion und Geschichte gefragt. Der Tod des Architekten Raimund Abraham am 4. März 2010 in Los Angeles gab den aktuellen Anstoß, diesen Wunsch einzulösen. Denn während es sicher noch einige Zeit dauern wird, bis das gesamte Œuvre Abrahams wissenschaftlich erfasst wird, scheint es wichtig, gerade diesen Bau, der zum bedeutendsten seiner Laufbahn wurde, jetzt in seinen verschiedenen Aspekten neu zu befragen. Wir freuen uns über die spontane Bereitschaft der Koautoren Peter Engelmann, Kenneth Frampton, Peter Marboe, Gerald Matt und Lebbeus Woods, zu diesem Tribut beizutragen, und bedanken uns auch beim Bauherren und Betreiber, dem österreichischen Bundesministerium für europäische und internationale Angelegenheiten, für seine großzügige finanzielle und organisatorische Unterstützung.

1	ACF und Fifth Avenue in Richtung Norden | View of ACF and 5th Avenue facing north
2	Fassade | Façade
3	Detail der Fassade | Detail of façade

3

Andres Lepik, Andreas Stadler

FOREWORD

In 1992, Raimund Abraham was the winner of the unique competition for the Austrian Cultural Forum New York's new building. And then began a difficult, but ultimately successful journey—both for the architect, who was living and teaching in New York, and for the Republic of Austria as commissioner and owner of the building. It was a brave decision to announce the competition publicly, to open it to all architects "of Austrian origin," and to leave the final decision up to a high-ranking international jury. The competition was Ernst Bliem's inspiration, and he has documented in detail how it was subsequently organized. The fact that this relatively small project—in comparison to the size of other buildings in Manhattan—was no sooner announced to the public than it was put on exhibit in The Museum of Modern Art, in 1993, was indicative of the special importance accorded to it from its inception.

Six years later, in 1999, after a phase when it almost seemed as if the project might fall through, the Architekturzentrum Wien (Architectural Center of Vienna) mounted the exhibition *Manhattan, Austria: The Architecture of the Austrian Cultural Institute by Raimund Abraham* in the Oval Hall of Vienna's Museum Quarter and published an exhibition catalogue that included information about the institution, the competition, and the architectural plans for the building. Soon thereafter the construction phase began, and, as expected, the complex design brought further challenges for all involved. The construction business in New York was not really set up to provide the precision and quality work required by the architect.

But the efforts made on all sides to realize the unique architecture of this structure have paid off. Since 2002, when the building opened to great international acclaim,

the Cultural Forum has become a popular destination for sightseers interested in architecture, and it also remains a magnet for architects themselves. Admirers of the building's design, and many members of the public who attend the events, have asked us again and again for a book about the history, function, and architecture of the building. It was the unexpected death of the architect, Raimund Abraham, on March 4, 2010 in Los Angeles that prompted us to write this book. It will certainly take some time for reviewing Abraham's entire oeuvre in depth, so there seems to be all the more reason now for us to focus on the various aspects of the Austrian Cultural Forum, which became the most important building of his career. We are pleased that our coauthors, Peter Engelmann, Kenneth Frampton, Peter Marboe, Gerald Matt and Lebbeus Woods, spontaneously agreed to write their tributes, and we wish to thank the commissioner and owner of this building, the Austrian Federal Ministry for European and International Affairs, for the generous support.

4   Detail der Fassade | Detail of façade
5   ACF und Nachbargebäude in Richtung Nordosten | View of ACF and surrounding buildings facing northeast

Andreas Stadler

DAS ÖSTERREICHISCHE KULTURFORUM NEW YORK: LEUCHTTURM UND TRÄGERRAKETE

2002: EIN PAUKENSCHLAG ZUR ERÖFFNUNG

Als im April 2002 New York und Österreich die Neueröffnung des Austrian Cultural Forum feierten, war allen an Kunst, Kulturpolitik und Architektur Interessierten klar, dass mit diesem Bau ein europäisches Land Neuland beschreitet und Geschichte schreibt. Noch waren die Wunden der Terroranschläge am 9. September 2001 nicht verheilt, schon sandte dieser markante Turm in Midtown Manhattan ein starkes Signal der Hoffnung an die Welthauptstadt des Geldes, der Kultur und der Medien aus.
Bürgermeister Michael Bloomberg erklärte den 18. April offiziell zum »Tag des Austrian Cultural Forum« und wies auf die verdienstvolle Rolle der Institution seit 1958 hin. Die außergewöhnliche Architektur und das zeitgenössische und innovative Programm seien eine Inspiration für die New Yorker Kunstszene. Die internationalen Medien staunten und lobten das kühne, visionäre Design seines Architekten Raimund Abraham, aber auch Österreichs Mut, sich mit zeitgenössischer Architektur und Kunstproduktion zu präsentieren. Die österreichische Architektur hatte wahrscheinlich seit Friedrich Kiesler nicht mehr so viel Beachtung in New York gefunden.
Hier stand sie nun: eine Architekturskulptur, die neben einer Galerie auf fünf Ebenen, einer Bibliothek auf zwei Stockwerken, Seminar- und Empfangsräumen mit fantastischer Aussicht auch Büros und Wohnungen bot. Was würde aus einem Kulturbau werden, dessen äußeres Erscheinungsbild in den Medien mit einer Guillotine, einer Rakete, einem Thermometer, Metronom und Dolch sowie mit einer modernen Version eines Osterinsel-Totems verglichen wurde?

6

7

8

9

Was würde aus einer Institution werden, die 1992 in einem einzigartigen offenen Architektenwettbewerb aufs Neue erfunden wurde? Wer hätte wohl gedacht, dass etwa zwanzigtausend Besucher pro Jahr dieses Gebäude und seine rund zweihundert Veranstaltungen, Konzerte, Debatten, Performances und Ausstellungen aufsuchen und dass Lehrer und Studenten von Design, Kunst und Architektur aus aller Welt auch nach Jahren noch an den regelmäßig angebotenen Führungen teilnehmen würden?

Nach fast zehn Jahren Betrieb kann das Kulturforum stolz auf seine starke Präsenz in den verschiedenen Kulturszenen und Medien hinweisen. Dies ist keinesfalls selbstverständlich, da sich das Programm in erster Linie auf die heutige zeitgenössische Kunst- und Wissensproduktion konzentriert und bewusst nicht das klassische österreichische Erbe zwischen Wolfgang Amadeus Mozart und Gustav Klimt instrumentalisiert.

Ein Blick in die Medienberichte bestätigt die Anerkennung der Ausstellungen, Konzerte und Debatten. Als ob das kantige Profil der Architektur auch auf das Programm abfärbte, wurden keine Experimente und heiklen Themen gescheut: mikrotonale Musik, Tanz und Performance als neue integrale Bestandteile des Programms, Todesstrafe, Orient und Okzident, World und Jazz als neue Klänge aus einem mittlerweile plurikulturellen Österreich, »Transversalität«, der Künstler als Störenfried, »Queer«, Geschlechter und Moderne, Herrschaftskritik und Kapitalismus, Nationalismus, Krieg, Europa und der »Ewige Frieden«.

Aber auch die Architektur wirkt weiter: 2009 etwa nahm der britische Reiseführer Wallpaper City Guide das Austrian Cultural Forum als einen der fünf wichtigsten Bauten New Yorks auf. Die Institution ist also einen weiten Weg gegangen.

NATIONALE KULTURREPRÄSENTATION VOR DER GLOBALISIERUNG

Zur Erinnerung: 1992 – im Jahr der Konzeption des neuen Gebäudes – war gerade erst der Eiserne Vorhang gefallen, und im ehemaligen Jugoslawien tobte der Bruder- und Bürgerkrieg. Österreich bereitete sich auf seinen Beitritt zur Europäischen Gemeinschaft vor, diskutierte, ob dies als neutrales Land überhaupt möglich wäre, und versuchte, den Demokratisierungs- und Transformationsprozess in Mittel- und Osteuropa zu unterstützen. Erst drei Jahre später, 1995, trat es der damals nur zwölf Mitgliedstaaten zählenden Europäischen Union bei.

Der Wettbewerb wurde also in einer Zeit ausgeschrieben, als das Wort Globalisierung noch nicht geläufig war, der Nationalstaat seine Repräsentation staatlich organisierte, eine Bibliothek das kulturelle Wissen und Erbe einer Nation fassen konnte, die internationale wissenschaftliche und kulturelle Zusammenarbeit relativ zentralisiert durch Ministerien organisiert, finanziert

und koordiniert wurde und als das Internet gerade die ersten Schritte machte, jedoch Telegramm und Telefax immer noch die schnellsten Kommunikationsmittel waren.

Niemand konnte wissen, wie sehr sich die Welt durch Globalisierung und Digitalisierung verändern würde. Auch der Architekt Raimund Abraham, dessen Projekt aus 226 Entwürfen als eindeutig bestes von einer unumstrittenen Jury ausgewählt wurde, konnte nicht ahnen, dass es zehn Jahre bis zur Vollendung des Bauwerks dauern würde. Rückblickend muss erwähnt werden, dass in den österreichischen Medien auch starke Kritik ob der hohen Baukosten laut wurde. Schlussendlich resümierte jedoch das *Wall Street Journal* 2002, dass die kolportierten Baukosten von 30 Millionen US-Dollar im Vergleich zum Innenausbau des Soho Prada Stores, der mit 40 Millionen US-Dollar zu Buche schlug, durchaus besser angelegt waren.

DIE WIEGE DER EMIGRATION

Das Forum konnte zu diesem Zeitpunkt bereits auf eine stolze Geschichte zurückblicken. Schon 1942 gründeten engagierte Österreicher, die von den Nazis vertrieben oder vor ihnen geflohen waren, ein Austrian Institute, dessen erste Aufgabe es noch während des Zweiten Weltkriegs war, die amerikanische Regierung und Öffentlichkeit für den Fortbestand von Österreich zu gewinnen. Nachdem 1938 viele österreichische Diplomaten in New York vom Deutschen Generalkonsulat übernommen wurden, fingen die Exil-Österreicher quasi bei null an und trafen sich in Cafés und Privatwohnungen zu Lesungen, Diskussionen und Konzerten. Dazu gehörten etwa die Schriftstellerin Mimi Grossberg, der einarmige Pianist Paul Wittgenstein, der ehemalige Bundesminister Guido Zernatto und die Antifaschistin Irene Harand. Auch Stefan Zweig beehrte diese Gruppe bei seinem Aufenthalt in New York, bevor er nach Südamerika weiterreiste.

An diese Institution knüpfte nun 1956 der junge Jurist und Übersetzer Wilhelm Schlag an, der mit dem Auftrag, ein Kulturinstitut zu gründen, noch mit dem Schiff nach New York reiste. Im Jahr 1958 erwarb die Zweite Republik in der 52. Straße das als Wohnhaus genutzte Stadtpalais des bekannten Geschäftsmannes Harley T. Proctor aus dem Jahre 1905. Daraufhin wurden nach Plänen der Architekten Carl Auböck und Eduard Sekler grundlegende Umbauarbeiten durchgeführt, die zum damaligen Zeitpunkt dem letzten Stand der zeitgenössischen Architektur und Kunst entsprachen. Damit wurde vom damaligen zuständigen Unterrichts- und Kulturminister Heinrich Drimmel, aber auch vom Staatssekretär und späteren Bundeskanzler Bruno Kreisky vor dem Hintergrund des Kalten Kriegs bewusst eine Annäherung an die USA verfolgt, die breit auf den Fundamenten des klassischen, des zeitgenössischen, aber auch des vertriebenen Österreichs basierte.

Der neue Direktor adoptierte den Namen Austrian Institute und arbeitete mit den Emigranten weiterhin eng zusammen, deren Organisation sich nun Austrian Forum nannte. Er selbst bewohnte auch – wie es damals generell üblich war – mit seiner Familie den Dachausbau und begann eine rege Veranstaltungstätigkeit im Haus mit Ausstellungen zeitgenössischer österreichischer Kunst, Lesungen und Konzerten. Gleichzeitig begann der ehemalige Leiter der österreichischen Fulbright-Kommission ein wissenschaftliches Netzwerk in den ganzen USA aufzubauen, das teilweise noch bis heute besteht.

Auch die nachfolgenden Institutsdirektoren Gottfried Heindl, Richard Sickinger und Fritz Cocron gingen den Weg der landesweiten Vernetzung weiter. 1976 organisierte die österreichische Bundesregierung zum Anlass der Zweihundertjahrfeiern der USA eine Jubiläumskollekte und sammelte genug Geld ein, um mit 1,5 Millionen US-Dollar an der University of Minnesota ein Center for Austrian Studies sowie an der Stanford University einen Österreich-Lehrstuhl einzurichten. Seither ist im Beirat beider Einrichtungen der amtierende Direktor des Kulturforums New York in beratender Funktion tätig. Die Zusammenarbeit mit diesen Einrichtungen sowie mit dem später gegründeten Center Austria an der University of New Orleans und dem Schumpeter-Fellowship-Programm an der Harvard University gehören bis heute zu den Aufgaben des Austrian Cultural Forum.

Vor allem unter den Direktoren Peter Marboe (1984 bis 1987), der zwischen 1991 und 1996 auch Leiter der kulturpolitischen Sektion im Außenministerium und damit auch für den Neubau verantwortlich war, und Wolfgang Waldner (1987 bis 1999) erfuhr die österreichische Auslandskulturpolitik eine substanzielle Aufwertung, die sich sowohl in der Zahl der Veranstaltungen, als auch im Budget niederschlug. Das 1999 erreichte Programmbudget konnte danach, auch im neuen Gebäude, nicht mehr erreicht werden. Dies soll hier jedoch nicht als Lamento verstanden werden, sondern als nüchterner Indikator dafür, dass sich der Nationalstaat in Zeiten der Globalisierung und Europäischen Integration – überall und nicht nur in Österreich – langsam aus dieser Identität stiftenden Funktion zurückzieht.

»TEN / TWENTY YEARS AFTER«: DAS AUSTRIAN CULTURAL FORUM AUFS NEUE ERFINDEN

Die Landkarte Europas hat sich verändert. 27 Staaten bilden nun die Europäische Union, und Österreich setzt sich nachhaltig für die Erweiterung um die verbleibenden Nachfolgestaaten des ehemaligen Jugoslawiens ein. Forschung wurde international zu einem entscheidenden Wettbewerbsfaktor, der sich immer mehr nationalen Strukturen entzieht. Auch Kunst und Kultur verorten und messen sich längst global entlang fein verästelter Disziplinen und passieren letztendlich jenseits staatlicher Strukturen der Auslandskulturpolitik. Folgerichtig nutzte der erste Direktor des neuen Hauses, Christoph Thun-Hohenstein, die Stunde und präsentierte ein Österreich heutiger Kreativität. Nach fünf Jahren Arbeit im neuen Haus konzedierte er: »Wir haben gelernt, dass großartige Architektur nicht automatisch Anerkennung bedeutet, wenn es um die Organisation kultureller Programme geht«. Mit dem medialen Schub des neuen Gebäudes wurde ein Feuerwerk zeitgenössischer Kreativität aus Österreich unter dem Titel *Transforming Modernity* vor allem in den Bereichen Musik und zeitgenössische Kunst losgelassen. Sensibel eingebettet in die europäisch-amerikanische definitorische Divergenz zwischen Moderne und Postmoderne konnte sich das Kulturprogramm auf der Höhe der Architektur behaupten.

Als zwischenzeitliches Fazit kann jedenfalls festgehalten werden, dass sowohl das Haus als »Leuchtturm« ausstrahlt als auch als Trägerrakete für die künstlerischen Karrieren von Hunderten von österreichischen Wissenschaftlern und Künstlern gedient hat und dient. In Zeiten der budgetären Engpässe und des Rückzugs des Staates aus kulturpolitischen Aufgaben muss sich die Institution immer wieder aufs Neue erfinden – um auch damit der Architektur gerecht zu bleiben. Raimund Abraham und die Republik Österreich als Bauherrin haben jedenfalls mit dem neuen Kulturforum nicht nur die architektonische Skyline Manhattans beeinflusst, sondern auch das österreichische Selbstverständnis als eine Nation zeitgenössischer Kreativität gestärkt.

6, 7	Büroräume | Staff offices
8	Bibliothek | Library
9	Fassade | Façade
10, 11	Eingang mit Ausstellungsplakaten | Entrance with exhibition posters
12	Austrian Institute, um 1963, Fassade | Austrian Institute façade, ca. 1963
13	Austrian Institute, um 1963, Erdgeschoss | Austrian Institute ground floor, ca. 1963
14	Veranstaltungsraum mit Flügel | Auditorium with grand piano
15	Veranstaltungsraum mit Technikraum | Auditorium with technical booth

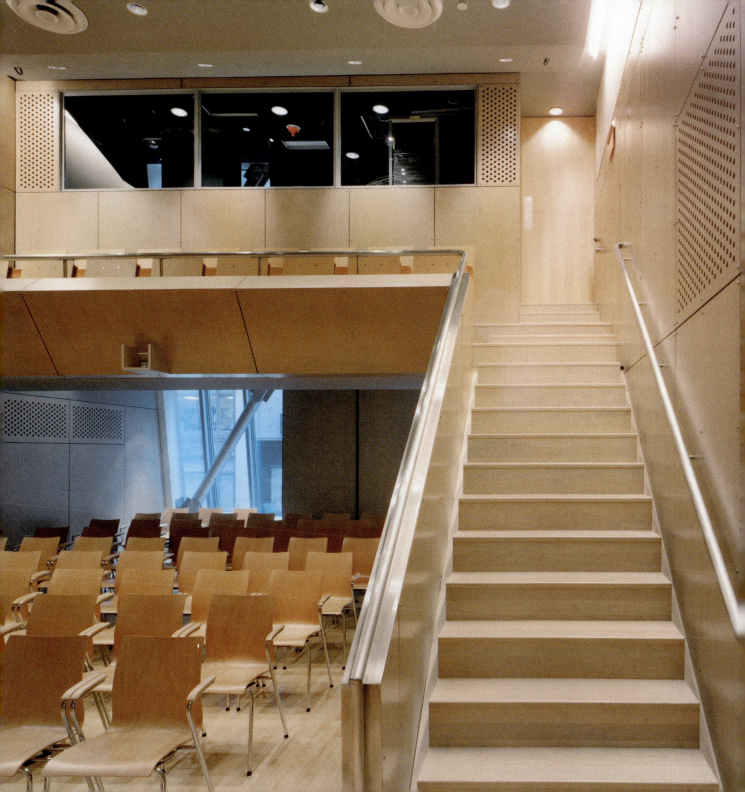

16–18 Ausstellungsansichten | Exhibition views *Under Pain of Death*
16 Lucinda Devlin, *Omega Suites*, 1991–1998, Lobby | lobby
17 Mathilde ter Heijne, *Menschen Opfern*, 2002, Hauptgalerie | main gallery
18 Steven Cohen, *SKULLETTOES*, 2006–2007, *Dead Man Dancing #12*, 2007, unteres Mezzanin | lower mezzanine

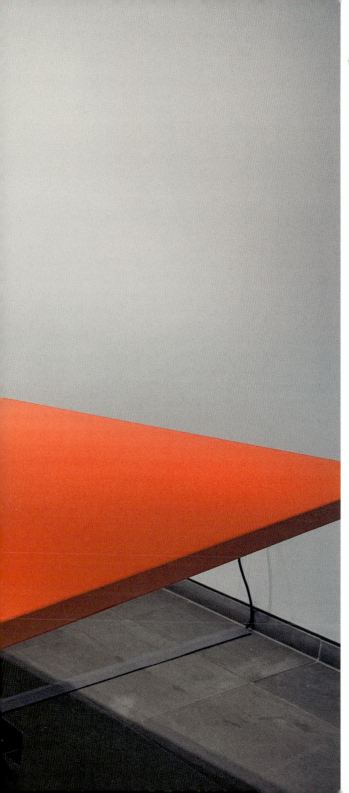

19 Ausstellungsansicht | Exhibition view *Bread and Soccer,* Serge Spitzer, *Global Culture (RED),* 2004–2005; Thomas Feuerstein, *Flesh for Fantasy,* 2008, unteres Mezzanin | lower mezzanine

20 Ausstellungsansicht | Exhibition view *Creative Migration,* Fotomontage mit Thom Fogarty | photomontage with Thom Fogarty, Anja Hitzenberger, *Thom I – IV,* 2009, unteres Mezzanin | lower mezzanine

21 Führung durch die Ausstellung *NineteenEightyFour,* unteres Mezzanin | Guided tour through the exhibition *NineteenEightyFour,* lower mezzanine

Andreas Stadler

THE AUSTRIAN CULTURAL FORUM NEW YORK: LIGHTHOUSE AND CARRIER ROCKET

2002: A SENSATIONAL OPENING

When New York and Austria celebrated the reopening of the Austrian Cultural Forum in April 2002, it was clear to everyone with an interest in art, culture, and architecture that a European country was breaking new ground and making history with this building. The wounds of the terrorist attacks on September 11, 2001 had not yet healed, but this distinctive tower in Midtown Manhattan was already sending out a strong signal of hope to the world capital of finance, culture, and media.

Mayor Michael Bloomberg officially declared April 18 the "Day of the Austrian Cultural Forum," mentioning the commendable role played by the institution since 1958. He called its remarkable architecture and its contemporary and innovative program an inspiration for the New York art world. The international media were amazed by the building and praised the bold, visionary design of its architect Raimund Abraham, but they also praised Austria's courage in presenting itself through the production of contemporary art and architecture. Austrian architecture had probably not been met with such respect in New York since Frederick Kiesler.

And now here it stood: an architectural sculpture that contained a gallery on five levels, a library on two floors, seminar rooms and reception rooms with fantastic views, and also offices and apartments. What would become of a cultural building whose external appearance was compared in the media with a guillotine, a rocket, a thermometer, a metronome, a dagger, and even a modern version of an Easter Island totem?

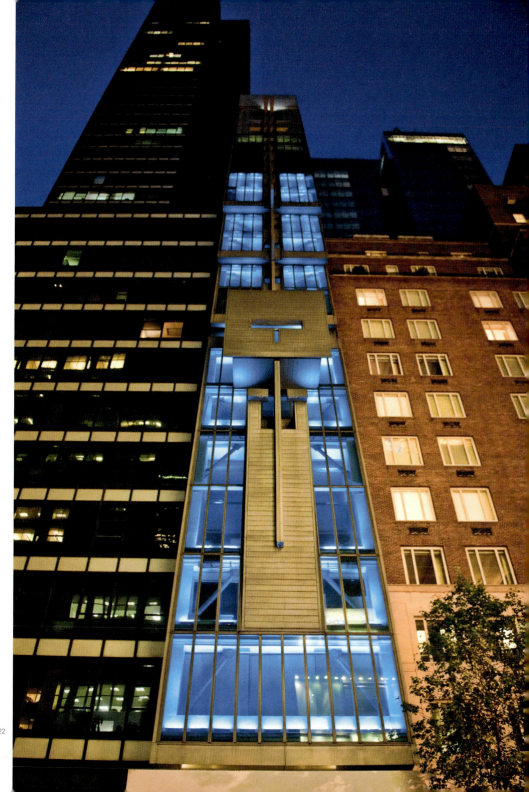

What would become of an institution that was reinvented in 1992 in a unique, open architectural competition? Who would have thought that approximately twenty thousand visitors a year would seek out this building to attend its approximately two hundred events, concerts, debates, performances, and exhibitions, and that teachers and students of design, art, and architecture from all over the world would still be taking the regularly offered guided tours?

After having now been in operation for almost ten years, the Cultural Forum can point proudly to its strong presence on the various cultural scenes and in the media. This was by no means a foregone conclusion, since the program concentrates primarily on the contemporary art being produced today and on new contributions to knowledge, deliberately not featuring the classical Austrian cultural heritage between the time of Wolfgang Amadeus Mozart and Gustav Klimt.

A look at the media reports confirms the recognition that the exhibits, concerts, and debates are receiving. As if the edginess of the architecture had also rubbed off on the program, we haven't shied away from any experiments or awkward topics: microtonal music, dance and performance as new integral components of the program, the death penalty, Orient and Occident, world music and jazz as new sounds from a now pluricultural Austria, "transversality," the artist as troublemaker, "queer," gender in the modern age, critique of domination and capitalism, nationalism, war, Europe and the "Ewige Frieden" ("Perpetual Peace").

But the architecture is also having a lasting effect: in 2009, for example, the British guidebook *Wallpaper City Guide* called the Cultural Forum one of the five most important landmarks in New York. So the institution has come a long way.

THE REPRESENTATION OF NATIONAL CULTURE BEFORE GLOBALIZATION

Let's remember that in 1992—the year of the architectural competition for the new building—the Iron Curtain had just fallen, and fratricidal civil war was raging in former Yugoslavia. Austria was preparing to join the European Union, discussing whether that was even possible as a neutral country, and trying to support the process of democratization and transformation in Central and Eastern Europe. It wasn't until three years later, in 1995, that it actually joined the European Union, which at that time had just twelve member states.

So the competition was announced at a time when the word "globalization" was not yet in common usage, when the nation-state organized its representation by state, when a library could hold the cultural knowledge and heritage of a nation, when international academic and cultural collaboration was organized, financed, and coordinated in a relatively centralized fashion by government departments, and when the Internet was just getting started, while telegram and fax were still the quickest means of communication.

22   Lichtinstallation *NYSTAGM* von Judith Fegerl, 2010, Fassade | Light installation *NYSTAGM* by Judith Fegerl, 2010, façade
23   Fassade während der Bauarbeiten | Façade construction
24   Eröffnungsfeier, 18. April 2002, Alois Mock (2. v. r.), Raimund Abraham (3. v. r.), Veranstaltungsraum | Opening ceremony, April 18, 2002; Alois Mock (seated second from right), Raimund Abraham (seated third from right), auditorium

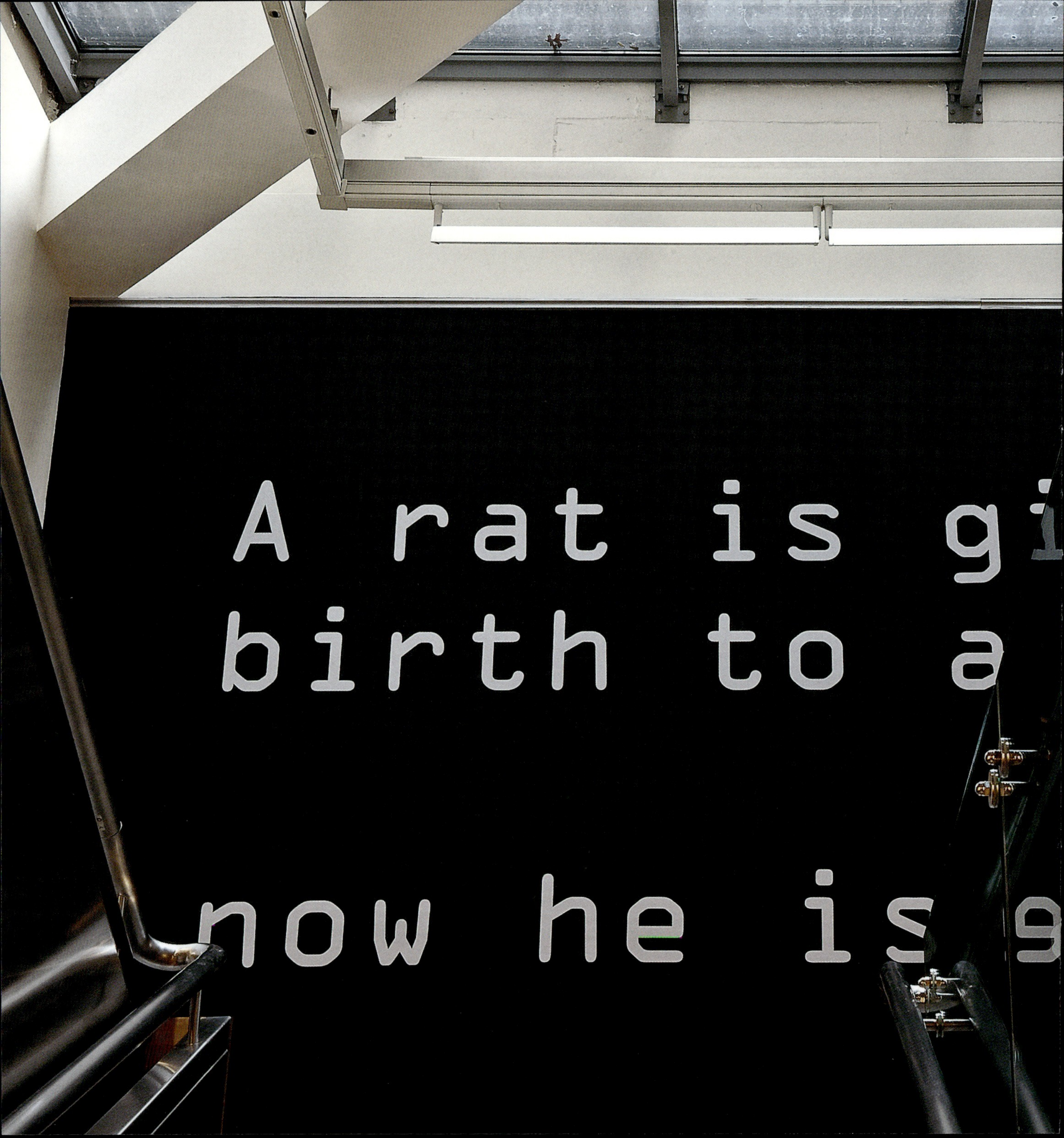

A rat is gi[ving]
birth to a

now he is g

25	Ausstellungsansicht	Exhibition view *Videorama*, Balam Bartolomé, *A Rat Is Giving Birth to a Man*, 2009, unteres Mezzanin	lower mezzanine
26	Jonas Mekas, Erhard Stackl, Andreas Stadler, Marina Abramović, Gerald Matt, Anna Jermolaewa (v. l. n. r.	from left to right), Veranstaltungsraum	auditorium
27	Ausstellungseröffnung *1989*, unteres Mezzanin	Opening reception for the exhibition *1989*, lower mezzanine

No one could know the extent to which globalization and digitalization would change the world. And the architect Raimund Abraham, whose project was unanimously judged to be the best of 226 entries, could not foresee that it would be ten years before the building was completed. In retrospect it should be mentioned that there was strong criticism voiced in the Austrian media about the high construction costs. But when the job was finished in 2002, *The Wall Street Journal* summed it up by saying that the rumored construction costs of 30 million U.S. dollars had been definitely better spent than the 40 million U.S. dollars it took to complete the interior of the Prada Store in Soho.

THE CRADLE OF THE AUSTRIANS IN EXILE

By this point in time, the Forum could already look back on a proud history. Back in 1942, politically involved Austrians, who had been driven out by the Nazis or had flown from them, founded an "Austrian Institute," whose primary task during the rest of the Second World War was to win over the American government and public for the continued existence of Austria. After many Austrian diplomats in New York were taken over by the German Consulate General in 1938, the Austrians in exile started virtually from scratch again, meeting in cafés and private apartments for readings, discussions, and concerts. Among them were the writer Mimi Grossberg, the one-armed pianist Paul Wittgenstein, the former Federal Minister Guido Zernatto, and the antifascist Irene Harand. And Stefan Zweig honored the group with a visit when he stayed in New York for a while before continuing on to South America.

In 1956, the young lawyer and translator Wilhelm Schlag sought contact with the group. He had traveled to New York by ship with instructions to found a Cultural Institute. In 1958, the Second Republic purchased the palatial city residence of the well-known businessman Harley T. Proctor on 52nd Street, built in 1905. After that, extensive renovations were carried out, according to plans by the architects Carl Auböck and Eduard Sekler, with art and architecture that was state-of-the-art at the time. With this project, which was implemented during the Cold War, the Minister for Education and Culture, Heinrich Drimmel, and also the Secretary of State and later Federal Chancellor, Bruno Kreisky, were actively seeking to improve Austria's relationship with the United States, a relationship based broadly on the fundamental principles of classical and contemporary Austria, but also of Austria in exile.

The new Director adopted the name "Austrian Institute" and continued working closely with the emigrants, whose organization was now called the "Austrian Forum." As was customary at the time, he and his family lived on the converted top floor, and he initiated an active program of events in

28–31 Ausstellungseröffnung *1989* | Opening reception for the exhibition *1989*
28 Franz Hackl, unteres Mezzanin | lower mezzanine
29 Veranstaltungsraum | Auditorium
30 Eröffnungsrede von Außenminister Michael Spindelegger, unteres Mezzanin | Speech by Austrian Foreign Minister Michael Spindelegger, lower mezzanine
31 Lobby | Lobby

28

29

30

31

the building, with exhibitions of contemporary Austrian art, readings, and concerts. At the same time, the former Director of the Austrian Fulbright Commission began to build up an academic network throughout the U.S., which is still partly operational today.

The following Directors of the Institute, Gottfried Heindl, Richard Sickinger, and Fritz Cocron, continued the efforts to form a network throughout the country. In 1976, on the occasion of the second centenary celebrations of the United States, the Austrian Federal Government organized a jubilee collection that brought in enough money to set up a Center for Austrian Studies at the University of Minnesota, and to establish an Austria Chair at Stanford University, providing 1.5 million U.S. dollars. Since then, the incumbent Director of the Cultural Forum New York has been active in an advisory capacity on the boards of both institutes. To this day, it is one of the tasks of the Austrian Cultural Forum to collaborate with these institutes, and also with Center Austria at the University of New Orleans, which was founded later, and with the Schumpeter Fellowship Program at Harvard University.

It was above all under Directors Peter Marboe (1984 to 1987) and Wolfgang Waldner (1987 to 1999) that the promotion of Austrian culture abroad was given a much higher priority. Peter Marboe was also Head of the Department of Culture in the Ministry of Foreign Affairs between 1991 and 1996 and thus responsible for pushing the construction of the new building through the Austrian domestic political process. The program budget of 1999 hasn't been equaled since, not even in the new building. This should not be taken as a lament, but rather as a sober indication that in the age of globalization and European integration, the national state—everywhere, not just in Austria—is slowly pulling back from the function of promoting its cultural identity.

32–35 Ausstellungsansichten *Verhüllen – Enthüllen: Der Schleier und die Kunst* | Exhibition views *The Seen and the Hidden: (Dis)Covering the Veil*

32 Marlene Haring, *Because Every Hair Is Different*, 2007, unteres Mezzanin | lower mezzanine

33 Ayad Alkhadi, *Structure I–III*, 2009; Sara Rahbar, *After You*, 2007, obere Galerie | upper gallery

34 Performance von Princess Hijab, Treppe des Mezzanins | Performance by Princess Hijab, mezzanine stairway

35 Ausstellungseröffnung, Treppe des unteren Mezzanins | Exhibition opening reception, lower mezzanine stairway

32

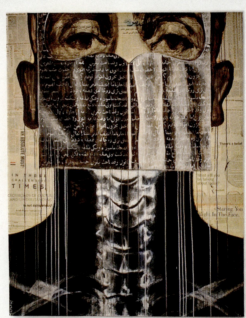

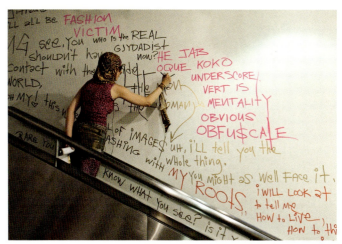

"TEN/TWENTY YEARS LATER": REINVENTING THE AUSTRIAN CULTURAL FORUM

The map of Europe has changed. Twenty-seven states now form the European Union, and Austria is making a sustained effort to have it expanded by the remaining succession states of former Yugoslavia. Research is increasingly freeing itself from national structures as it moves onto the international playing field. Art and culture are also undergoing a repositioning and have long since been competing globally as the disciplines branch out. They too have moved beyond the state structures that promote our culture abroad. Consequently, the first Director of the new building, Christoph Thun-Hohenstein, took the opportunity to hightlight Austria's contemporary creativity. After five years of working in the new building, he conceded: "We have learned that although a great building is an asset, it doesn't necessarily earn you automatic recognition as an organizer of cultural programs beyond the realm of architecture." With the media attention on the new building, there was a fireworks display of contemporary creativity from Austria entitled "Transforming Modernity," above all in music and contemporary art. With sensitivity for the divergence between European and American definitions of modernism and postmodernism, the cultural program attained the same level of recognition as the building itself.

As an interim report, we can say with certainty that the building is shining like a lighthouse and also that it has served and continues to serve as a carrier rocket, launching the artistic careers of hundreds of Austrian scholars and artists. In times of budgetary restraint, and with the state de-emphasizing the promotion of its culture abroad, the institution has to reinvent itself time and again—to do justice to the architecture in this regard as well. Both Raimund Abraham and the Republic of Austria, which commissioned and owns the new Cultural Forum, have not only influenced the architectonic skyline of Manhattan but have also strengthened Austria's conception of itself as a nation of contemporary creativity.

36 Ausstellungseröffnung *Solace*, unteres Mezzanin | Opening reception for the exhibition *Solace*, lower mezzanine

Andres Lepik

GEGEN DEN STROM

In den Hochhausschluchten Central Manhattans sticht das Austrian Cultural Forum als ein architektonischer Fremdkörper ins Auge. Obwohl nur 24 Stockwerke hoch und gerade einmal 7,6 Meter breit, tritt es mit seiner kaskadenartig nach oben abgestuften Fassade aus Zinkblech und Glas kraftvoll in den Stadtraum. Die weit vorkragenden Bauelemente und tiefen Einschnitte lassen den Bau zugleich skulptural, archaisch und rätselhaft erscheinen: Er verweigert die einfache Lesbarkeit seiner Funktionen und regt zu manchen Vermutungen an. Eines ist sofort klar: Diese scharfkantige Architektur sucht keinen jovialen Schulterschluss mit ihren Nachbarn, sondern entwickelt ihr Profil aus dem kalkulierten Kontrast. Es ist eine Fassade, die sich mit aller Entschiedenheit gegen den Strom der üblichen Glas- und Stahlfassaden stemmt. Unter der Herrschaft des Internationalen Stils hatte sich auch in Manhattan in der zweiten Hälfte des 20. Jahrhunderts eine immer stärkere Angleichung der Hochhausbauten etabliert. Die Mehrheit dieser austauschbaren Kisten – und daran änderte auch das historisierende Dekor der Postmoderne nur wenig – erfüllte vor allem eine Funktion: die der optimalen kommerziellen Verwertbarkeit. Architektur im Sinne der Gestaltung eines kulturellen Mehrwerts durch ein Bauwerk blieb die Ausnahme. Als daher die Republik Österreich im Jahre 1992 den Neubau seines Kulturzentrums an der 52. Straße nach den Plänen von Raimund Abraham ankündigte, erkannte die lokale Architekturkritik bereits in dem veröffentlichten Projekt eine bedeutende Inspiration für die Architekturlandschaft Manhattans. Eine so starke Reaktion, wie es dieses Projekt hervorrief, konnte nur einer auslösen, der die architektonische Situation dieser Stadt gut genug kannte und zugleich frei von den üblichen Verflechtungen und Zwängen war.

37

DER ARCHITEKT

Raimund Abraham wurde 1933 in Lienz, Osttirol, geboren und studierte Architektur an der Technischen Universität Graz. Nach kurzer Tätigkeit als Architekt in Österreich übernahm er 1964 eine Professur an der Rhode Island School of Design in Providence und siedelte in die Vereinigten Staaten über. 1971 wechselte er an die Cooper Union School of Architecture in New York und

37 Raimund Abraham, Wohn- und Geschäftshaus, Berlin | Raimund Abraham, residential and office building, Berlin

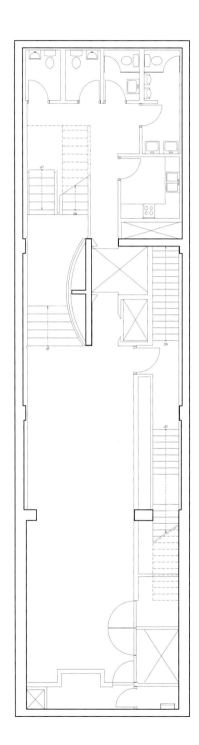

Die Hauptgalerie (1. Untergeschoss) ist ein 150 m² großer Raum. An der Nordseite befinden sich Besuchertoiletten und eine Küche, auf der südlichen Seite ein verdeckter Lastenlift. | The main gallery (level -1) is a 1,600-square-foot space. At the north side are public restrooms and a catering kitchen; at the south side is a concealed elevator opening to the sidewalk.

wurde zugleich Professor am Pratt Institute. 2003 wurde er auch Fakultätsmitglied am Southern California Institute of Architecture (SCI-Arc). Abraham, der die letzten Jahre in New York und in Mazunte, Mexiko, lebte, starb am 4. März 2010 in Los Angeles. Er trennte seine Arbeit in Forschung und Praxis, wobei gerade in der ersten Zeit in den USA sein Schwerpunkt fast ausschließlich auf der Forschung lag. Zwischen 1961 und 1964 arbeitete er an den »Compact Cities«, gezeichneten Visionen monumentaler Architekturmaschinen, und den «Transplantational Cities«, Collagen und Fotomontagen von beweglichen Strukturen, teils auch als fantastische Implantate im Kontext Manhattans. New York war ein Ort, der für ihn von Anfang an eine besondere Herausforderung für die Entwicklung seiner Ideen darstellte.

Abraham stellte sich mit seinen Ideen und Entwürfen konsequent gegen die funktionalistischen Dogmen der Moderne. Mit dieser Kritik stand er zu Beginn der 1960er-Jahre nicht allein. An mehreren Orten zugleich entwickelten sich neue Ansätze, die weniger nach der konkreten Umsetzbarkeit als nach der Ausprägung neuer, originärer Denkrichtungen in der Architektur fragten: In England war dies die Gruppe Archigram, in Japan die der Metabolisten. Und in Österreich, speziell in Wien, bildeten sich mit Laurids Ortner, Wolf Dieter Prix, Hans Hollein, Walter Pichler, Gernot Nalbach sowie einigen anderen experimentelle Gruppierungen wie Haus-Rucker-Co und Coop Himmelb(l)au, die nach neuen Grundlagen und Perspektiven für die Architektur forschten. All diese Bewegungen suchten nach neuen Visionen, nach einer Architektur, die das Künstlerische und die Imagination wieder mit einbezog. Abraham bildete in diesem Kontext eine Art Außenposten, aber auch einige der Wiener Kollegen kamen nach New York, wie etwa Hans Hollein, der 1967 bis 1969 einen Galerieumbau für Richard L. Feigen durchführte, oder die Mitglieder von Haus-Rucker-Co, die von 1970 bis 1977 ein Büro in der Stadt unterhielten. Schon 1967 stellte Abraham mit Hans Hollein und Walter Pichler in der Ausstellung *Architectural Fantasies* erstmals im Museum of Modern Art aus und wurde damit einer weiteren Öffentlichkeit in New York bekannt.

Ab den 1970er-Jahren wandte sich Abraham in seinen Studien von der Untersuchung der Stadt der Betrachtung des Einzelhauses als Grundtypus der Architektur zu. Das »Imaginary House« wurde in zehn Variationen zu einem zentralen Element seiner kolorierten Entwürfe. Die radikalste Ausprägung darunter war das »House without Rooms«. Neben solchen poetischen Architekturstudien beschäftigte sich Abraham auch mit spezifischen, urbanistisch besonders markanten Orten wie Venedig (»Nine Projects for Venice«, 1979/80) oder Berlin (»Kirche an der Berliner Mauer«, 1982). Für die Internationale Bauausstellung (IBA) in Berlin errichtete Abraham 1980–1987 ein Wohn- und Geschäftshaus an der südlichen Friedrichstraße (siehe S. 46). Dieser Bau lässt bereits deutlich seine radikale Entwurfshaltung in der Praxis erkennen, denn er verweigert jegliche Anpassung durch eine konventionelle Fassade und behauptet seine eigene, expressiv-skulpturale Qualität.

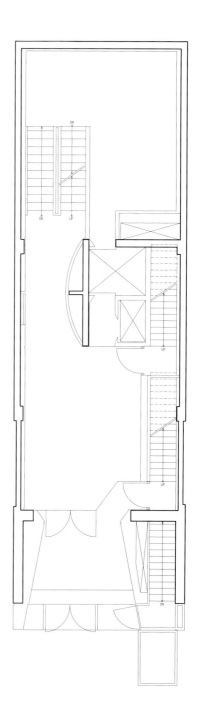

Der Haupteingang befindet sich an der 52. Straße. Besucher gelangen über die freitragende Treppe in die obere Galerie. | The main entrance is situated on East 52nd Street. Moving down the floating staircase, visitors reach the upper gallery.

Nach diesem Bau in Berlin nahm Abraham mit Erfolg an einigen international wichtigen Wettbewerben teil. In den Wettbewerben für die Erweiterung des Jüdischen Museums in Berlin (1988) erhielt er den zweiten, in dem für das Akropolis-Museum in Athen den dritten Platz (1990). Mit dem Gewinn des ersten Preises im Wettbewerb für den Neubau des Österreichischen Kulturinstituts in New York rückte Abraham 1992 ins Zentrum der internationalen Aufmerksamkeit. Ähnlich wie Daniel Libeskind und Zaha Hadid wurde ein weiterer Architekt, der vor allem durch seine utopischen Entwürfe bekannt war, nun mit einem wichtigen Bau beauftragt. Und nach jahrzehntelanger Abwesenheit von Österreich avancierte Abraham auf einmal zum wichtigsten Repräsentanten der österreichischen Architektur im Ausland. 1993 konnte er sein siegreiches Projekt für das Kulturinstitut im Museum of Modern Art ausstellen, ein Zeichen der Anerkennung und auch der starken Unterstützung, die er schon vor der Ausführung für dieses Projekt erhielt.

DER BAU

Das vorgegebene Raumprogramm für das Austrian Cultural Forum war sehr komplex. Für die Öffentlichkeit zugänglich sollten eine Lobby, Ausstellungsflächen, ein Auditorium, eine Bibliothek und Seminarräume untergebracht werden. Darüber hinaus mussten auch noch mehrere nicht öffentliche Büros, Gästewohnungen und die repräsentative Wohnung des Direktors Platz finden. Dazu kamen noch die vorgeschriebenen Feuertreppen, zwei Aufzugsschächte und die technische Versorgung. Zu den zentralen Entwurfsideen Abrahams gehörte die Verlagerung der Feuertreppe auf die Rückseite des Gebäudes. Damit konnte die Gebäudetiefe in der vollen Breite ausgenutzt werden. Die doppelläufige Feuertreppe bildet die von Abraham sogenannte »Wirbelsäule« des Baus, hinter dem Raumkern der vierundzwanzig Geschosse. Der Fluchtweg aus den oberen Etagen muss zwar, wie baupolizeilich vorgeschrieben, auf die Vorderseite zur Straße hin geleitet werden, doch geschieht dies auf der ersten und zweiten Etage an der Brandwand der Ostseite entlang.
Die Galerie für Wechselausstellungen ist schon vom Eingang an der Straße aus einsehbar und öffnet sich vom Erdgeschoss auf zwei Ebenen nach unten und oben. Ein Oberlicht an der Rückseite der in das Grundstück durchgeschobenen Lobby gibt den Blick auf die hohe Rückwand der Feuertreppen frei. Durch die Sichtbeziehungen von der Straße durch die Lobby hindurch in den von Tageslicht erleuchteten Ausstellungsraum und den nach oben geleiteten Blick wird der Eindruck von Weite und räumlicher Offenheit erreicht. Der Ausstellungsraum zieht sich im Untergeschoss noch tief bis unter den Gehsteig der Straße hindurch und nutzt das Maximum des baulich Möglichen aus. Vom ersten Treppenabsatz nach oben führt eine weitere Treppe zum Veranstaltungsraum mit achtundsiebzig Sitzplätzen, der sich ebenfalls

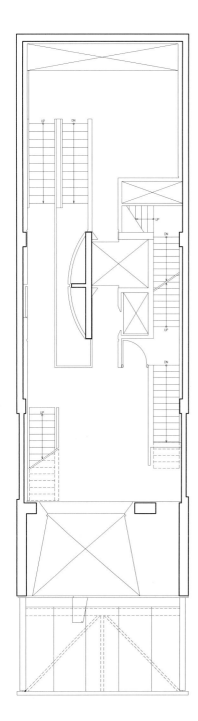

Vom Erdgeschoss aus erreichen Besucher über eine Treppe das untere Mezzanin, welches mit dem oberen Mezzanin durch eine schlanke Brücke verbunden ist. Weitere Treppen führen in den Veranstaltungsraum. | Ascending the stairs from ground level, visitors reach the lower mezzanine that connects via a sleek bridge to the upper mezzanine. Another flight of stairs leads to the auditorium.

über zwei Etagen erstreckt. Darüber liegt im vierten und fünften Obergeschoss die Bibliothek. Auf dem siebten Stockwerk folgt das Büro des Direktors, das zur Straße hin, hinter der so auffällig vorkragenden Wandscheibe, aus einem großen quadratischen Raum besteht. Aus den Seitenfenstern bietet sich ein einmaliger Ausblick auf die Manhattan quer durchschneidende Schlucht der 52. Straße. In den darüberliegenden Stockwerken befinden sich weitere Büros der Mitarbeiter sowie auf fünf Etagen die Wohnung des Direktors mit einem Speisezimmer und, auf der zwanzigsten Etage, einer begehbaren Dachterrasse.

Die innere Organisation des Baus ist von hoher Funktionalität. Auf engster Fläche sind die unterschiedlichen Nutzungsansprüche an ihrem jeweils besten Ort platziert und sinnvoll miteinander verknüpft. Die innere Struktur folgt jener Ästhetik von Hochleistungsmaschinen, aus denen Abraham einen Teil seiner Inspiration bezog: »Im Gegensatz zu den Futuristen, die Maschinen als fortschrittbringendes Heilmittel betrachteten, stellen sie für mich Konstrukte äußerster Präzision und zielführender Logik dar.« Dass Abraham dabei dieser »Maschine« eine expressive Fassade gab, die er selbst als »Maske« bezeichnete, weist auf ein anderes seiner zentralen Anliegen: der Architektur eine Gestaltung zu verleihen, die unverwechselbar und wiedererkennbar bleibt.

Das Austrian Cultural Forum hat in Manhattan genau jene architektonische Signalwirkung erlangt, die im Wettbewerb des Jahres 1992 eine der zentralen Forderungen an die beteiligten Architekten war. Innen wie außen beweist es, wie viel hochwertig gestaltete Architektur aus einer kleinen Baulücke herauszuschlagen ist, wenn es nicht nur darum geht, kommerziellen Verwertungsansprüchen zu folgen: »Here we encounter the idea that patrons should serve culture, not the other way around« (Herbert Muschamp). Das Austrian Cultural Forum löst damit zwei Ansprüche zugleich ein, die in New York über Jahrzehnte kaum noch zu finden waren: architektonische Identität und Qualität. Seine Identität gewinnt es aus der bewussten Verankerung in jenen antimodernen Ansätzen, die in New York über lange Jahre auch von John Hejduk oder Lebbeus Woods in der Forschung und Lehre repräsentiert wurden, die aber in der Gestalt der Stadt bis dahin keinen Niederschlag gefunden hatten. Das Austrian Cultural Forum ist das bedeutendste Bauwerk in Abrahams Karriere geworden und zugleich eines jener wenigen architektonischen Manifeste, die die Wahrnehmung für die gebaute Realität Manhattans verändert haben.

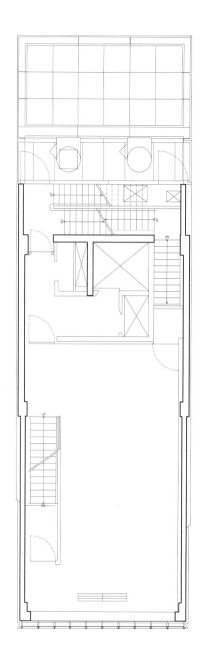

Der Veranstaltungsraum befindet sich im 2. und 3. Stock. Ein Hauptmerkmal hier ist das Podest, das den Flügel vertikal bewegt. | The auditorium occupies levels 2 and 3. A key feature of the auditorium is a mobile platform for a grand piano, adjustable from floor to ceiling.

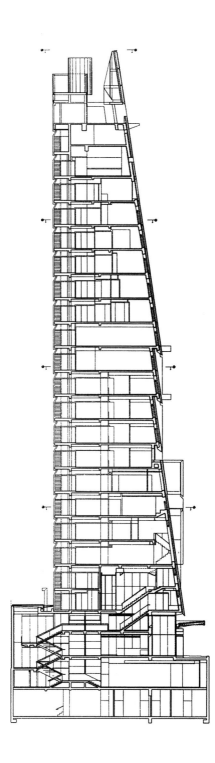

38 Schnitt | Section

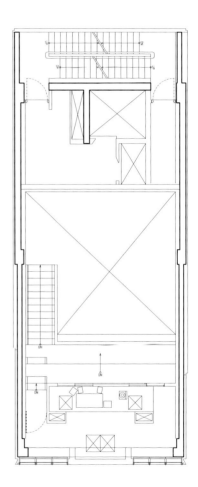

Der 3. Stock beherbergt den hochmodernen Technikraum, der unter anderem Projektionen, Aufnahmen und Fernsehübertragungen ermöglicht. | Level 3 houses the technical booth. It contains state-of-the-art communications systems, facilitating projection, recording, and broadcasting.

Andres Lepik

AGAINST THE TIDE

Among the high-rises that line the narrow streets of Central Manhattan, the Austrian Cultural Forum stands out as an architectural anomaly. Although it is only twenty-four stories high and just twenty-five feet wide, its layered façade of zinc and glass cascading upward fosters a powerful impression in the city. The wide protruding components and the deep recesses lend the building something that is at once sculptural, archaic, and puzzling: its function is not obvious, which leads to some speculation. One thing is immediately clear: this sharp-edged architecture does not seek to rub shoulders jovially with its neighbors, but develops its profile from the calculated contrast. It is a façade that sets itself with great determination against the trend of the conventional glass and steel façades. The predominance of the International Style during the second half of the twentieth century is evident in Manhattan, where the high-rise buildings began to resemble each other more and more closely. The majority of these interchangeable boxes—and even the historicizing postmodern décor did little to change this—had just one function: to be as commercially profitable as possible. "Architecture," in the sense of creating surplus cultural value through a building, remained the exception. Therefore, when the Republic of Austria announced in 1992 that it had chosen a design by Raimund Abraham for a new building for its Cultural Center on 52nd Street, local architectural critics recognized right away that the publicized project represented a significant inspiration for the architectural landscape of Manhattan. Only an architect sufficiently familiar with the architectonic situation in the city, while at the same time free of the usual involvements and restrictions, could call forth such a strong reaction.

THE ARCHITECT

Raimund Abraham was born in Lienz, East Tirol, in 1933 and studied architecture at the Technische Universität Graz (Graz University of Technology). After working for a brief time as an architect in Austria, he accepted a professorship at the Rhode Island School of Design in Providence and moved to the United States. In 1971, he transferred to the Cooper Union School of Architecture in New York and became an adjunct professor at the Pratt Institute. In 2003,

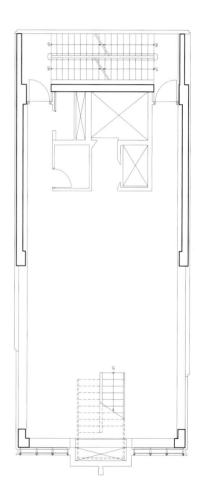

Im 4. und 5. Stock sind die Bibliothek und der Lesebereich. Die beiden Stockwerke sind mit Innentreppen verbunden. | Levels 4 and 5 of the building hold the library and reading area. These two levels are connected by interior stairways.

he moreover became a faculty member at the Southern California Institute of Architecture (SCI-Arc). In recent years, Abraham lived in New York and in Mazunte, Mexico, and he passed away on March 4, 2010, in Los Angeles. He separated his work into research and practice, with the main emphasis, particularly in his early years in the States, being almost exclusively on research. Between 1961 and 1964 he worked on his "Compact Cities," drawn visions of monumental architectural machines, and on his "Transplantational Cities," collages and photomontages of moveable structures, some of which were fantastical implants in the context of Manhattan. From the very beginning, New York was a place that presented him with a particular challenge for the development of his ideas.

With his ideas and designs, Abraham consistently opposed the functionalist dogmas of modernism. At the beginning of the nineteen-sixties, he wasn't alone in his criticism. New approaches to architecture arose spontaneously in several places, approaches that were less concerned with concrete realization than with the formation of original new ways of thinking: in England it was Archigram, in Japan the Metabolists. And in Austria, especially in Vienna, Laurids Ortner, Wolf Dieter Prix, Hans Hollein, Walter Pichler, and Gernot Nalbach were among those who formed experimental groups such as Haus-Rucker-Co and Coop Himmelb(l)au that sought to change the basic structures and perspectives of architecture. All of these movements were looking for new visions, for an architecture that once again included artistry and imagination. In this context, Abraham formed a sort of outpost, but some of his Viennese colleagues came to New York too, for example Hans Hollein, who reconstructed a gallery for Richard L. Feigen between 1967 and 1969, or the members of Haus-Rucker-Co, who had an office in the city from 1970 to 1977. As early as 1967, Raimund Abraham, Hans Hollein, and Walter Pichler had their first exhibition in The Museum of Modern Art. Entitled *Architectural Fantasies*, it brought them to the attention of a wider public in New York.

In the seventies, Abraham turned his attention away from the city as a field of study and began to contemplate the free-standing house as the prototype of architecture. The "Imaginary House" became a central element of his colored drawings. Of his ten variations on this theme, the most radical was the "House without Rooms". In addition to such poetic architectural studies, Abraham also made plans for specific places with particularly striking features of urban development, such as Venice ("Nine Projects for Venice," 1979–80) or Berlin ("Kirche an der Berliner Mauer" [Church by the Berlin Wall], 1982). For the Internationale Bauausstellung (IBA), or International Building Exhibition, which took place in Berlin from 1980 to 1987, Abraham erected a combined residential and office building at the corner of Friedrichstrasse and Kochstrasse (see p. 46). His radical approach to design and his refusal to conform are already clearly evident in this building, where he asserted his own expressive, sculptural quality in the unconventional façade.

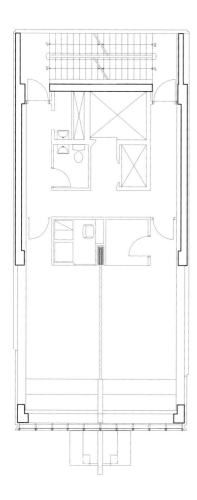

Im 6. Stock befindet sich ein loftartiger Konferenz- und Seminarraum, der mit einem Vorhang geteilt werden kann. | Level 6 holds a loft-like conference and seminar space, which can be divided by a curtain.

After constructing this building in Berlin, Abraham competed successfully in several important international competitions. He won second prize in the competition for the extension of the Jüdisches Museum (Jewish Museum) in Berlin (1988), and third prize in the competition for the Acropolis Museum in Athens (1990). After having won first prize in the competition for the new Austrian Cultural Forum in New York in 1992, Abraham became the center of international attention. As with Daniel Libeskind and Zaha Hadid, yet another architect who was known primarily for his utopian designs had now received the commission for an important building. And although it had been decades since he had lived in Austria, Abraham suddenly became the most important representative of Austrian architecture abroad. The fact that he was able to exhibit his winning project for the Cultural Forum in The Museum of Modern Art in 1993 was an indication of the recognition and the strong support he received even before the building was begun.

THE BUILDING

The predetermined distribution of space for the Austrian Cultural Forum was very complex. The public was to have access to a lobby, exhibition areas, an auditorium, a library, and seminar rooms. But there also had to be rooms that were closed to the public: offices, guest apartments, and the Director's prestigious apartment. And there still had to be the regulation fire escapes, two elevator shafts, and all the necessary technical equipment. One of the central ideas of Abraham's design was to locate the fire escape on the back of the building, so that the full width of the building's interior could be used to its best advantage. The double stairs of the fire escape are situated behind the core space with its twenty-four floors, forming what Abraham called the "vertebra" of the building. The building code stipulates that the escape route from the upper floors must come around to the side facing the street, so these stairs emerge to the front along the firewall on the east side, at the level of the first and second floors.
The gallery for temporary exhibitions is partially visible from the street through the entrance. From the main floor, it opens out onto two levels above and two below. The lobby runs the length of the building, with a window high up at the back that offers a clear view of the high outside wall of the fire escape. By means of the relationship between the views from the street, through the lobby, and into the exhibition room, which is illuminated by daylight that directs one's gaze upward, Abraham has created the impression of width and openness. The exhibition room continues out under the sidewalk to the full extent that is architecturally possible. From the landing halfway up the first flight of stairs, another staircase leads up to the seventy-eight seat auditorium, which likewise extends over two floors of the building.

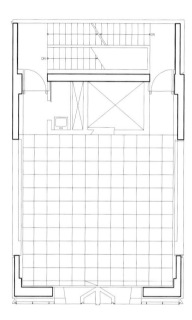

Auf dem 20. Stock befindet sich eine Dachterrasse. Sie bietet einen einzigartigen Ausblick durch die Häuserschluchten Manhattans in Richtung Westen zum Hudson und in Richtung Osten zum East River. | Level 20 is occupied by a roof terrace. It offers sensational views across Manhattan's urban canyons, to the Hudson River in the west, and all the way to the East River in the east.

Above it, on the fourth and fifth floors, is the library. On the seventh floor, behind the wall plate that stands out so conspicuously, is the Director's office, a large, square room facing the street. From the side windows, there is a unique view down onto 52nd Street that cuts across Manhattan. On the floors above, there are more offices for the staff, and also the five-floor apartment with dining room for the Director. And on the twentieth floor there is a roof terrace.

The interior organization of the building is highly functional. In the narrowest area, each of the various usage requirements is in its best possible position and meaningfully linked to the others. The interior structure is governed by the aesthetics of high-performance machinery, from which Abraham derived part of his inspiration: "In contrast to the Futurists, who saw machines as signs of progress and the answer to our ailments, I see them as designs of utmost precision and goal-oriented logic." The fact that Abraham gave this "machine" an expressive façade, which he himself called the "mask," points to another of his central concerns: giving architecture a distinctive form that remains recognizable.

The Austrian Cultural Forum has achieved exactly that striking architectural effect in Manhattan which was one of the main requirements for the architects who took part in the competition in 1992. On the inside and out, it proves how effectively high-quality architecture can leap up from a small empty site when commercial viability is not the sole deciding factor: "Here we encounter the idea that patrons should serve culture, not the other way around" (Herbert Muschamp). So the Austrian Cultural Forum simultaneously meets two criteria that were conspicuously absent in New York for decades: architectonic identity and quality. Its identity is intentionally anchored in the antimodern school of thought that was represented in New York for years in the research and teaching of Raimund Abraham, John Hejduk, and Lebbeus Woods, but that had not previously been reflected in the appearance of the city. The Austrian Cultural Forum has become the most significant building of Abraham's career and, at the same time, one of the few architectural manifestos to have changed the way people perceive the built reality of Manhattan.

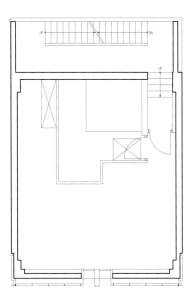

Der 21. sowie die darüberliegenden Stockwerke stehen für Technik wie Maschinenräume, das Fensterreinigungssystem und den Wassertank zur Verfügung. | Levels 21 and higher are devoted to technical functions, including machine rooms, the window cleaning system, and the building's water tower.

RAIMUND ABRAHAM IM GESPRÄCH MIT GERALD MATT

8. SEPTEMBER 2009

GERALD MATT: Neulich habe ich eine Dokumentation über die Häuser von Architekten gesehen. Unter anderem auch über ein Haus, das Du Dir in Mexiko gebaut hast und das noch im Bau war. Wie ist das Verhältnis zwischen Architektur und Landschaft bei Dir? Was steht da dahinter?

RAIMUND ABRAHAM: Vor etwa fünfzehn Jahren bin ich das erste Mal in diese Gegend – eine Reihe von Fischerdörfern – gekommen. Ich war auf einer Tempelexkursion und wollte eine Woche ans Meer fahren. Auf der Landkarte habe ich nach der unzugänglichsten Küste gesucht und so diese Gegend entdeckt, dann dort Freundschaften geschlossen und bin seitdem jedes Jahr wieder gekommen. Nach einer gewissen Zeit ist mir dort vor allem abgegangen, dass ich nicht selbst kochen konnte. Der Herd ist ja die Seele eines Hauses. Nicht die Hütte war der Ursprung der Architektur, sondern das Feuer. Dazu gibt eine sehr schöne Legende von Reyner Banham, einem Architekturkritiker aus den 1960er-Jahren, die erzählt, wie eine Gruppe von urzeitlichen Jägern auf eine Lichtung kam, auf der Äste lagen. Nun mussten sie die Entscheidung treffen, ob sie mit den Ästen eine Hütte bauen oder Feuer machen sollen. Sie haben sich entschieden, Feuer zu machen. Das ist der Ursprung der Architektur: nicht das Gebäude, sondern das Ereignis, das die Architektur bestimmt. Schlafen kann man auch unter einem Baum. Ich dachte nie daran, für mich selbst ein Haus zu bauen. In der Zeit, die ich dort verbrachte, beobachtete ich immer, wie die Menschen dort leben und wohnen. Entscheidend sind zwei ökologische Kräfte, die die Bewohnbarkeit ermöglichen: Schatten und Wind. Ich entwickelte ein Gebäude mit einer dominanten Dachstruktur, die Schatten erzeugt und zugleich den Wind vom Meer auffängt und in das Hausinnere weiterleitet. Es steht auf einem Hügel mit Blick aufs Meer, etwa fünfhundert Meter vom Meer entfernt.

GM: War diese Entfernung wichtig?

RA: Ja, sehr wichtig, denn um die Landschaft zu kontemplieren, muss man Intimität bewahren. Wenn man zu nah am Meer ist, wird die Aussicht – also die visuelle Erfahrung – so dominant, dass man ihr ausgeliefert ist. Darum ist diese Distanz ganz entscheidend.

GM: Ist das ein Moment, der bei anderen Bauten auch eine Rolle spielt? Ich denke zum Beispiel an das Kulturinstitut in New York, das hättest du ja rein theoretisch aus einer einzigen Glasfassade machen können.

RA: Na ja, da spielen wieder andere Kräfte eine Rolle. In Midtown Manhattan sind die Häuser wesentlich größer als das projizierte und zulässige Volumen des neuen Gebäudes. Daher galt es, ein Bauwerk zu schaffen, das trotz seiner Kleinheit die Größe der anderen Gebäude infrage stellt. Die Schmalheit des Gebäudes war ja vorgegeben, das war die Herausforderung und letztlich die Essenz meines Entwurfs. Jeder Ort bietet eine andere Herausforderung und daher glaube ich, dass in der Architektur die Transformation eines Ortes wichtiger ist als das Gebäude selbst. Der Ort ist für mich entscheidend. Martin Heidegger hat den etymologischen Ursprung dafür gefunden: Die älteste althochdeutsche Wurzel für das Wort »Ort« bedeutete »Spitze einer Lanze«. Das heißt, die Spitze einer Lanze kann man entweder mit der Spitze nach oben aufrecht in die Sonne richten, wo sich die ganze Energie sammelt und reflektiert, oder man dreht sie um, stößt sie in die Erde und nimmt dadurch Besitz von der Erde. Das heißt, es ist ein Punkt, den man definiert und der den Ort bestimmt. Dagegen sind die meisten der jetzigen Häuser ortlos, zu Grundstücken degradiert.

GM: Wenn man Architektur und Landschaft in ein Verhältnis setzt, gibt es Strategien der Anpassung oder der Veränderung. Wenn Du Architektur machst, habe ich das Gefühl, ist das bereits Ersetzen.

RA: Es kann nie Anpassung sein. Ich glaube, jeder Eingriff in einen Ort muss radikal sein. Das ist die fatale Konsequenz der Architektur: Man verletzt einen Ort. Man verletzt den Horizont. Und sogar die Zeichnung selbst ist schon ein Eingriff. Das Papier wird zum Ort und die Zeichnung wird zur Transformation des Ortes. Architektur zu entwerfen ist also ein Versöhnungsprozess.

GM: Soll Architektur Deiner Meinung nach auch eine gewisse Form von Unzulänglichkeit haben?

RA: Das finde ich schon. Es muss in der Architektur die Freiheit geben, ein Haus zu bauen, in das kein Licht eindringen kann – als Resultat eines bewussten Prozesses. Wenn man das Fenster vergisst, dann ist das Ignoranz.

GM: Wie hast Du das bei Deinem neuesten Projekt bei Düsseldorf gelöst?

RA: Mein letztes im Bau befindliches Gebäude ist ein Haus für Musiker auf der ehemaligen Raketenstation Hombroich. An diesem von einer militärischen Strategie geplanten Ort wollte ich ein Gebäude schaffen, das völlig nach innen orientiert ist. Also einen Raum schaffen, der nach außen von einer kreisförmigen Wand, die das Innere schützt, bestimmt wird und sich nur zum Himmel öffnet. Ich hatte das Gefühl, dass ein Raum, in dem musiziert wird, geschützt sein muss. Wenn man die Landschaft sehen möchte, muss man hinaustreten. Im Gegensatz zu der zum Klischee gewordenen Glasarchitektur.

GM: Wobei das ja später auch mit den technischen Möglichkeiten zu tun hatte ...

RA: Am Anfang der Moderne war man natürlich fast verpflichtet, alle neuen technischen Errungenschaften zu verwenden, die dann die Formsprache der Architektur veränderten. Mit den heutigen unbegrenzten technologischen Möglichkeiten, Ideen baulich umzusetzen, muss man sich wieder auf die Wurzeln des Bauens besinnen. Mich interessiert zum Beispiel mehr, in unserer Zeit mit elementaren Baustoffen neue räumliche Möglichkeiten zu realisieren.

GM: Dazu wollte ich schon zu Beginn unseres Gesprächs etwas fragen: Du bist ja aus Lienz und lebst jetzt in New York und Mexiko, bist viel unterwegs als Lehrer, Künstler, also ein Weltbürger. Du sprichst aber auch immer wieder die Architektur in den Bergen an, die traditionelle Architektur der Bauern. Welche Rolle hat diese alpine Bauweise für Dich gespielt?

RA: Eine ganz entscheidende. In den frühen 1960er-Jahren, als meine ersten radikalen Architekturprojekte entstanden – also in einem Moment der Befreiung von den Normen des Berufsarchitekten –, erschien mein Buch *Elementare Architektur* im Residenz-Verlag. Nach dem Abschluss des Architekturstudiums sah ich die Qualität von Bauten, mit denen ich seit meiner Kindheit vertraut war. Ohne Mies van der Rohe und Le Corbusier hätte ich diese Einsicht wahrscheinlich nicht gehabt, denn diese Erfahrung hat sicherlich meine Rezeption geändert. Die wirkliche Entdeckung besteht nicht darin, dass man neue Landschaften sucht, sondern dass man neue Augen bekommt. Ich wollte diese Bauten nicht historisch dokumentieren, sondern ihre Anonymität respektieren. Diese Bauten wurden gefunden, unvorbereitet und überraschend, wodurch die Authentizität des Anonymen gewahrt werden konnte. Es war eine Entdeckungsreise mit meinem Freund Josef Dapra, der mit dem Auge der Kamera die essenzielle Qualität dieser Bauten festhielt und sozusagen meine Vision übersetzte.

GM: Wie entwickelte sich das weiter? Es gab dieses Buch, dann irgendwann mal Architektur, aber auch Zeichnungen und sehr viel Theorie. Wie hängt das alles zusammen?

RA: In meinen Zeichnungen und meiner gebauten Architektur setze ich mich mit haptischen und nicht mit optischen Räumen auseinander. Zeichnen und Bauen sind für mich nicht eine Erscheinung, sondern ein Ereignis, das jegliche Spekulation zu überwinden versucht. Wenn ich über das, was ich gezeichnet und gebaut habe, rede, werde ich genauso zum Spekulanten wie jeder Historiker, jeder Theoretiker. Alles, was ich jetzt sage, ist retrospektiv. Man könnte sagen, was immer ich zu sagen habe oder jetzt sage, hat nichts mit meiner Arbeit zu tun.

GM: Was passiert aber, wenn eine Zeichnung umgesetzt wird? Für Dich hat die Zeichnung einen Eigenwert. Und das Gezeichnete muss nicht unbedingt realisiert werden, weil es bereits Architektur ist. Kann man das so sagen?
RA: Absolut. Architektur muss nicht gebaut werden.
GM: Du unterscheidest auch immer zwischen gezeichneter und gebauter Architektur.
RA: Ja, natürlich. Wenn ich weiß, dass ich etwas baue, zeichne ich ganz wenig. Ich mache ein paar Skizzen. Wenn die Idee da ist, baue ich sofort Modelle. Zum Kulturinstitut in New York gibt es vielleicht fünf Skizzen, dafür aber riesige Modelle. Übrigens steht das ganz große, sechs Meter hohe Modell verpackt im Keller des Wien Museums. Wenn ich also eine Idee zeichne, denke ich immer 1:1. Auch bei meinen kompliziertesten imaginären Projekten denke ich immer, wie sie konstruiert sind – also konstruiert im metaphorischen Sinn. Aber wenn ich beispielsweise mein gezeichnetes »Haus mit Vorhängen« bauen sollte, würde ich mich weigern, weil es für mich notwendig wäre, dass die Vorhänge, so wie ich sie gezeichnet habe, immer vom Wind bewegt werden. Das ist ein Beweis, ein Beispiel dafür, dass die gezeichnete Architektur genauso wirklich wie die gebaute ist. Eine Zeichnung und alle Phasen des Bauens gehören dem Architekten. Ein fertiges Bauwerk gehört sich selbst.
GM: Ist das nicht auch ein bisschen der Unterschied zwischen Utopie und Realität? Ich meine, die Zeichnung erlaubt alles, die bauliche Umsetzung ist dann ganz anders.
RA: Ich habe nie utopisch gedacht. Für mich ist alles wirklich. Dass die Zeichnung alles erlaubt, ist ein Fehlschluss. Die Architekturzeichnung ist von einer metaphorischen Konstruktion bestimmt, die übersetzbar ist, aber nicht übersetzbar sein muss. Eine Linie muss die Latenz besitzen, eine Kante zu werden und Lagen von Pigmenten, die Vorahnung einer materiellen Oberfläche. Nur dann ist eine Übersetzung einer Zeichnung möglich. Eine Computerlinie ist keine wirkliche Linie, sondern das Bild einer Linie, und eine Computerzeichnung ist das Bild eines Bildes.
GM: Gab es irgendwelche architektonischen oder geistigen Ideen, die Dich fasziniert haben?

RA: Als ich Walter Pichler traf, verspürte ich die Notwendigkeit, die Architektur, wie ich sie kannte, infrage zu stellen, das heißt, mich vom Beruf des Architekten zu lösen, während Pichler sich von der Grafik und Skulptur trennen wollte und wir beide Ideen entwickelten, die zu einer neuen Architektur führen sollten. Ohne Vorbilder, doch inspiriert von den Flaktürmen in Wien, peruanischen Tempeln und unbekannten Landschaften.
GM: Du hast mehrmals den Begriff »radikal« verwendet. Mir fällt auf, dass »radikal« ein Terminus ist, den die Generation dieser Zeit sehr gerne verwendete. Heute ist man diesem Begriff gegenüber ein bisschen skeptisch geworden, weil er in vielen Zusammenhängen verwendet worden ist, wo er eigentlich fast entwürdigt wurde.
RA: Man kann auch statt radikal kompromisslos sagen, es ist vielleicht ein präziseres Wort. Was ich auch als radikal bezeichne, ist die Fähigkeit, Widerstand zu leisten gegen das, was offensichtlich ist. Und unsere Zeit ist eine offensichtliche Zeit. Es ist alles offensichtlich. Und darum ist es auch viel schwieriger, heutzutage radikal zu sein, weil man einen Gegner haben muss, um Widerstand zu leisten. Und wenn der Gegner nicht mehr bekannt ist, ist es äußerst schwierig, Widerstand zu leisten. Das heißt, dann kann man nur sich selbst als seinen eigenen Gegner betrachten, der man ja auch ist, und dadurch kann man nur innerhalb dieser Auseinandersetzung arbeiten. Ich muss also zu mir selbst radikal sein und nicht zu anderen. Es ist alles möglich. Es ist niemand mehr überrascht.
GM: Das ist für Dich ein wesentlicher Unterschied zwischen der heutigen Zeit und den 1960er-Jahren?
RA: Es geht um den Verlust einer geistigen Haltung, um den Verlust des Willens zum Widerstand, des Widerstands gegen die Moden und der bedenkenlosen Bewunderung alles Neuen. Kunst ist zum Marktprodukt geworden, und Künstler zu Händlern, Ausstellungsmacher zu Kuratoren.
GM: Das ist aber ein sehr tiefes Hinterfragen einer der Kriterien der Moderne, die letztlich ausschließlich aus Innovation besteht.
RA: Die radikalste Erfindung der Moderne war ja nicht nur, sich mit Geschichte auseinanderzusetzen, also Geschichte zu verneinen, sondern die eigentlichen Wurzeln

der Sprache infrage zu stellen und dadurch eine neue Grammatik, eine neue Etymologie zu erfinden. Heute ist die Kunstsprache zum Esperanto geworden, also eine Allgemeinsprache, die alle sprechen und deren Wurzeln niemand mehr begreift.

GM: Der Versuch ist aber gescheitert. Wenn wir auf Dein Buch aus den 1960er-Jahren zurückkommen: Was an diesen Ideen oder Thesen hat für Dich persönlich noch Gültigkeit?

RA: Thesen sind austauschbar, das Werk niemals.

GM: Und würdest Du manchen der Ideen, die Du in dem Buch geäußert hast, so etwas wie Allgemeingültigkeit zurechnen? Es hat ja immer ein bisschen Manifestcharakter, wenn ein Künstler ein Buch macht.

RA: Was bleiben muss, ist die Haltung, die die Arbeit bestimmt.

42

39–41 Details der Fassade | Details of façade
42 Blick aus einem Fenster im 6. Stock in Richtung Süden | View through a window on the 6th floor facing south

RAIMUND ABRAHAM IN CONVERSATION WITH GERALD MATT

SEPTEMBER 8, 2009

GERALD MATT: I recently saw a documentary film about the houses architects live in. One of the houses it showed was a house you had built for yourself in Mexico, which was still under construction at the time the film was made. How do you see the relationship between architecture and landscape? What's at the root of it?

RAIMUND ABRAHAM: I first discovered the place about fifteen years ago—the coast is dotted with fishing villages. I was on a temple excursion and wanted to spend a week by the ocean. So I got out the map and looked for the most inaccessible part of the coast, and that's how I discovered the place. Now I've made friends there and go back every year. After a while what I really missed was that I couldn't cook. The hearth is the soul of a house. Architecture didn't originate with a hut; it originated with fire. The English architectural critic Reyner Banham wrote a beautiful legend about that in the nineteen-sixties: A group of primeval hunters entered a clearing and saw some branches lying on the ground. Then they had to decide if they should use the branches to build a hut or to make a fire. They decided to make the fire. And that was the origin of architecture.

It's not the building that determines the architecture, but the event. We can sleep just as well under a tree. I never thought of building a house for myself. In the time I spent there, I kept noticing how the indigenous people live and what kind of houses they have. There are two ecological forces of prime importance in making that landscape livable: shade and wind. So I developed a building with a dominant roof structure that creates shade and at the same time catches the wind from the ocean and causes it to blow into the inside of the house. It's on a hill with a view of the ocean, but back from the shore by about 500 meters, or over 1,600 feet.

GM: The distance was important?

RA: Yes, very important, because if you want to contemplate the landscape, you have to keep things intimate. If you're too close to the ocean, the view—the visual experience—is so dominant that you're overpowered by it. That's why it's so important to be some distance back.

GM: Is that a determining factor in your other buildings as well? I'm thinking, for example, of the Austrian Cultural Forum in New York. Theoretically, that could have had a solid glass façade.

RA: Well, there were other factors at play there. In Midtown Manhattan, the surrounding buildings were substantially larger than the projected and permissible volume of the new building. So the challenge was to create a building that, in spite of being smaller, would challenge the dimensions of the other buildings. It was stipulated from the start that the building would be narrow—that was the challenge and ultimately the essence of my design. Every place offers a different sort of challenge, and that's why I think that in architecture the transformation of a place is of greater importance than the building itself. For me, the place is the deciding factor. Heidegger found the etymological origin of this word: the oldest Old High German root of the word *Ort* or "place" means "the spearhead of a lance." If you think about it, the spearhead of a lance can either be held upright, with the tip of it gathering and reflecting all the energy from the sun, or it can be inverted and driven down into the earth to stake a claim, in which case it's a point you define that

determines the place. By way of contrast, most buildings today have no sense of place; they've been degraded to mere pieces of property.

GM: When you establish a relationship between architecture and landscape, there are strategies of adaptation or alteration. I have the feeling that the architecture you design is a form of replacement.

RA: It can never be adaptation. I think that every intrusion on a place is radical. That is the unfortunate consequence of architecture. It violates a place. It violates the horizon. Even an architectural drawing is an intrusion. The paper becomes the place and the drawing becomes the transformation of the place. So the designing of architecture is also a process of reconciliation.

GM: Do you think architecture should allow for some departures from the norm?

RA: Yes, I do. An architect should have the freedom, for example, to construct a building that lets in no light at all—as the result of a conscious thought process. Of course, if he simply forgets the windows, that's ignorance.

GM: How did you solve that in your most recent project, near Düsseldorf?

RA: My most recent building under construction is a music studio on the former Hombroich Missile Base. In this place, which was planned by military strategy, I wanted to create a building that's oriented entirely toward the inside. That is, to create a space that is defined to the outside by a circular wall that protects the inside and opens only toward the sky. I had the feeling that a room where music is made has to be protected. If you want to see the landscape, you have to go outside. It's the opposite of the glass architecture that's become so commonplace.

GM: Although that also came about because of technological advances . . .

RA: When modern architecture was in its beginnings, people of course felt obliged to use all of the new technological developments, which in turn changed the formal language of architecture. Today, with unlimited technological means of converting ideas into structures, we have to remind ourselves again of the basics of building. For example, in our time, I'm more interested in using elemental building materials to realize new spatial possibilities.

GM: I wanted to ask you something about that right at the beginning of our conversation: you're from Lienz, Austria, and now you live in New York and Mexico. You're much in demand as a teacher and an artist, so you travel a lot and have become a citizen of the world. Yet you refer again and again to the architecture in the mountains, the traditional architecture of farmers. What role has this alpine method of building played in your work?

RA: A very decisive role. In the early sixties, at the same time as my first radical architectural projects came into being—a time of liberation from the norms of the professional architect—I coauthored the book entitled *Elementare Architektur: Architectonics* (Elemental Architecture: Architectonics) that was published by Residenz in 1963. It wasn't until after I had graduated as an architect that I recognized the quality of the buildings that had been familiar to me since my childhood. Without Mies van der Rohe and Le Corbusier, I probably would not have had that insight. This experience certainly changed my way of looking at things. True discoveries are not made by looking for new landscapes; they are made when you change your way of looking at things. I didn't want to document the history of these buildings, but rather to respect their anonymity. I simply came across these buildings, unprepared and surprised, which is how I was able to preserve the authenticity of the anonymous people who built them. I had gone exploring with my friend Josef Dapra, who captured the essential quality of these buildings with his camera, thereby transferring my vision onto paper, so to speak.

GM: What did that lead to? There was the book, but then at some point there was architecture. There were also drawings, and there was a lot of theory. How is all that connected?

RA: In my drawings and in the architecture I have built I deal with haptic rather than optic spaces. I think of drawing and building not as an appearance, but rather as an event that attempts to overcome any speculation. When I talk about what I have drawn and built, I become just as speculative as every historian, every theorist.

Everything I'm saying now is retrospective, and it could be maintained that whatever I have to say or what I'm saying now has nothing to do with my work.

GM: But what happens when a drawing is turned into a building? For you, the drawing has a value of its own. And what is drawn doesn't necessarily have to be realized, because it's already architecture. Have I understood you correctly?

RA: Yes, absolutely. Architecture doesn't have to be built.

GM: You always make a clear distinction between drawn architecture and built architecture.

RA: Yes, of course. When I know that I'm going to build something, I don't make very many drawings. I make a few sketches. Once the idea is there, I immediately start building models. For the Austrian Cultural Forum in New York there are perhaps five sketches, but there are huge models of it. Incidentally, the gigantic model that is six meters or twenty feet high is packed up in storage in the basement of the Wien Museum in Vienna. So when I draw an idea, I always think in a ratio of 1:1. Even with my most complicated imaginary projects, I'm always thinking of how they're constructed—that is, constructed in the metaphorical sense. But if someone told me to build my drawn "House with Curtains," for example, I would refuse, because for me, the curtains would always have to be the way I drew them, blown by the wind. So there's proof for you, an example that drawn architecture is just as real as built architecture. A drawing and all the phases of its construction belong to the architect. A finished building belongs to itself.

GM: Isn't that rather like the distinction between utopia and reality? What I mean is that in the drawing everything is possible, whereas its realization as a building is something else altogether.

RA: I've never been a utopian thinker. For me, everything is real. It's simply not true that everything is possible in the drawing. The architectural drawing is determined by a metaphorical construct that can be realized, but doesn't have to be. A line has to have the latent ability to become an edge, and layers of pigment have to have the presentiment of a material surface. Only then is it

possible to realize a drawing. A line in a computer isn't a real line, it's the picture of a line, and a computer drawing is the picture of a picture.

GM: Were there any architectonic or intellectual ideas that fascinated you?

RA: When I met Walter Pichler, I felt the need to question architecture as I knew it, that is, to get out of the profession. And it turned out that Pichler wanted to get away from graphic art and sculpture, and the two of us were developing ideas that would lead to a new architecture. We weren't modeling ourselves on anyone, but we were inspired by the anti-aircraft towers in Vienna, by Peruvian temples, and by unknown landscapes.

GM: You've used the word "radical" several times. It occurs to me that the present generation is very fond of the word radical, although we've become a little skeptical of it, because it has been used in so many contexts that it's become hackneyed.

RA: Instead of "radical" you can also say "uncompromising." That may be a more precise word. What I mean by radical is the ability to offer resistance to what is obvious. And we live in an obvious time. Everything is obvious. And that's why it's all the more difficult to be radical nowadays, because you have to have an opponent in order to offer resistance. And when you don't even know who the opponent is, it's extremely difficult to offer resistance. In that case, you just have to regard yourself as your own opponent, which is what you are anyway, and then you work by having this ongoing debate with yourself. So I have to be radical toward myself, and not toward others. Everything is possible. No one is surprised anymore.

GM: Do you see that as an essential difference between today and the nineteen-sixties?

RA: What's been lost is an intellectual stance; people have lost the will to resist things, to resist fashions, and to resist the unhesitating admiration of everything that's new. Art has become a marketable product, artists have become dealers, and people who prepare exhibitions have become curators.

GM: You're being very skeptical about one of the main criteria of modernism, which after all consists entirely of innovation.

RA: The most radical idea of modernism wasn't just to take issue with history, to negate history, but rather to call into question the actual roots of the language and thereby to come up with a new grammar, a new etymology. Today, the language of art has become Esperanto, a general language that everyone speaks, and no one understands its roots anymore.

GM: But the attempt failed. Let's go back to your book from the sixties: Which of those ideas or theses do you personally still consider valid?

RA: Theses are interchangeable—the work of art never is.

GM: Would you say that some of the ideas you expressed in the book have something like universality? It's always a little like a manifesto when an artist writes a book.

RA: What has to remain is the stance that determines the work.

43	ACF in Richtung Nordosten | View of ACF facing northeast
44	Treppe in der Bibliothek | Stairway in the library
45	Blick aus einem Fenster im 7. Stock in Richtung Südosten | View through a window on the 7th floor facing southeast
46	Büroraum | Staff office
47	Detail der Treppenstruktur | Detail of stairway structure

Peter Engelmann

RAIMUND ABRAHAM: EIN POSTMODERNER DENKER UND DEKONSTRUKTIVISTISCHER ARCHITEKT

Das Austrian Cultural Forum in New York ist nach rein architektonischen Maßstäben ein überaus gelungenes Projekt. Interessant ist dieses Gebäude aber nicht allein wegen seiner formalen Lösungen, sondern wegen seines stimmigen, freien und unbefangenen Umgangs mit den es konstituierenden Elementen. Raimund Abrahams umfassender charismatischer Ansatz, der Architektur in den Mittelpunkt einer gesellschaftlichen Diskussion stellt, sowie seine Weltläufigkeit und seine Vernetzung mit den Strömungen der zeitgenössischen Architektur sind in einem Entwurf zusammengeführt, aus dem »eines der seit Jahrzehnten interessantesten Gebäude in Manhattan« entstand, wie es die *New York Times* formulierte.

Schon 1986 hatte Abrahams verkündet, Form interessiere ihn nicht als solche, sondern nur, »wenn sie aus einem Prozess von Ereignissen zustande kommt«. Architektur ist in diesem Verständnis nicht die Anwendung eines Prinzips oder einer abstrakten Idee von einem Gebäude, sondern Resultat eines kreativen Prozesses, der in der Auseinandersetzung mit den determinierenden Elementen eine Lösung sucht.

Abraham war nicht einfach ein österreichischer Architekt, dem gegen Ende seiner Karriere dann endlich ein so bedeutendes Stück Architektur gelang. Angefangen von seiner Emigration 1964 nach Amerika bis hin zur Aufgabe seiner Staatsangehörigkeit aus Protest gegen die schwarz-blaue Regierung war Abraham stets ein unabhängiger Geist, der nicht das tat, was man von ihm erwartete, sondern das, was er für richtig hielt und wofür er sich engagierte. Durch seine Weltläufigkeit war er früh mit internationalen Tendenzen und Theorien vertraut. Welcher österreichische Architekt außer ihm sprach 1986 über Maurice

Blanchot? Während man im Glauben, das sei internationales Niveau, in Wien unsägliche postmoderne Gebäude an den Ring oder die Radetzkystraße setzte, war Abraham ein entschiedener Gegner der Postmoderne in der Architektur und denunzierte deren Populismus als faschistische Tendenz. Die Pointe dieser Gegnerschaft ist jedoch, dass er gegen die Architekturpostmoderne mit den Argumenten der philosophischen Postmoderne zu Felde zog. Die Postmoderne, wie sie der französische Philosoph Jean-François Lyotard 1979 in seinem berühmten Buch *Das postmoderne Wissen* begründete, hatte einen Kerngedanken: Allgemeine Prinzipien, Abstraktionen, die Lyotard »große Erzählungen« nannte, dürfen die konkreten Interessen und Ziele der Menschen nicht mehr überdeterminieren und in der Theorie und der Praxis nicht mehr Ausgangspunkt und leitendes Prinzip sein, sondern sie sind allenfalls Resultat einer Bewegung, die von unten nach oben geht. Auf jedem Gebiet kommt es darauf an, die konkrete Situation zu erfassen, vorurteilslos zu analysieren und zum Ausgangspunkt für Lösungen zu nehmen. Das gilt für die Politik genauso wie für die Philosophie oder eben auch für die Architektur.

»Das Blatt Papier ist für mich der Ort und Architektur ist für mich Eingriff in den Ort«, sagt Raimund Abraham über sein Entwerfen. Aus einer solchen elementaren Aktion entwickelt sich der Entwurf und formuliert ein neues Bedeutungssystem. Mit dieser Entwurfstechnik zeigt Abraham noch eine zweite, auf den ersten Blick nicht erkennbare Verwandtschaft. Denn die Aufwertung des elementaren, voraussetzungslos von signifikantem Material ausgehenden Entwurfprozesses gegenüber der Tradition der Bedeutungsapplikation auf ein Konkretes ähnelt stark den zentralen Einsichten der Dekonstruktion. Dekonstruktivistische Architektur heißt nicht, dass man ungerade Linien baut, sondern sie entsteht, wenn der Architekt den Prozess der architekturalen Bedeutungsproduktion aus elementaren Bestandteilen zulässt.

Der Umstand, dass Raimund Abraham Österreich früh verlassen hat, war für seine Arbeit gewiss prägend. Seine eigenständigen, im Umgang mit den avanciertesten Architekten und Architekturtheoretikern herausgebildeten Überzeugungen vom voraussetzungslosen, die Vielfalt des Gegebenen verarbeitenden Entwerfen und die Vehemenz, mit der er seine Ansichten vertreten hat, haben mit dem Austrian Cultural Forum einen Rahmen für die Präsentation österreichischer Kultur geschaffen, der eben nicht nur Rahmen ist, sondern – ganz im Sinne der zeitgenössischen Philosophie und Kulturtheorie – selbst Bedeutung generiert. Das Gebäude zwingt zu hoher Disziplin und Kohärenz der kulturellen Programmierung, weil es sich selbst nur mit seiner intellektuellen Stringenz und seinem klaren Konzept in der kraftvollen Umgebung all der architekturhistorisch aufgeladenen Gebäude in Midtown Manhattan behaupten kann. Das Gebäude ist auf der Höhe der Zeit. Indem es auf jeden historischen Zitatenkitsch verzichtet, sich aus sich heraus entfaltet und in einen Dialog mit seiner Umgebung tritt, verkörpert es programmatisch die Idee eines Kulturforums.

Peter Engelmann

RAIMUND ABRAHAM: A POSTMODERN THINKER AND DECONSTRUCTIVIST ARCHITECT

By purely architectonic standards, the Austrian Cultural Forum in New York is a project that turned out extremely well. But this building is interesting not just because of its formal solutions, but also because of the harmonious, free, and natural way it deals with its constituent elements. Raimund Abraham's comprehensive, charismatic approach makes architecture the main topic of a societal discussion. He is also cosmopolitan and interconnected with the trends of contemporary architecture. The combination of these characteristics in his design resulted in "one of the most exciting New York buildings in decades," as stated in *The New York Times*.

Back in 1986, Abraham announced that form as such didn't interest him, that it is only interesting "when it comes into being from a sequence of events." Architecture in this sense is not the application of a principle or of an abstract idea of a building, but rather the result of a creative process that seeks a solution through working with the determining elements.

Abraham wasn't just an Austrian architect who finally succeeded in having a very significant piece of architecture built toward the end of his career. From the time of his emigration to America in 1964, right through to his renunciation of his citizenship out of protest against the Austrian "People's Party and Freedom Party" coalition government, Abraham was always an independent spirit who chose to do not what was expected of him, but what he considered correct and what he was committed to. Because of his cosmopolitanism, he was acquainted early on with international tendencies and theories. What Austrian architect other than Abraham was talking about Maurice Blanchot in 1986? While people were erecting unspeakable postmodern

buildings in Vienna on the Ring or on Radetzky Street, in the belief that they were conforming to an international standard, Abraham was a decided opponent of the postmodern in architecture and denounced its populism as a fascist tendency. The main thing about that opposition, though, is that he crusaded against architectural postmodernism with the arguments of philosophical postmodernism. Postmodernism, as founded by the French philosopher Jean-François Lyotard in 1979 in his famous book *The Postmodern Condition: A Report on Knowledge*, had one central idea: general principles, abstractions that Lyotard called "grand narratives," can no longer be permitted to overdetermine people's concrete interests and goals, and can no longer be the point of departure and the guiding principle in theory and practice; instead, they are at best the result of a movement that goes from the bottom to the top. In every field, the important thing is to comprehend the concrete situation, to analyze it without bias, and to take it as the starting point when looking for solutions. That's true for politics, just as it is for philosophy, or for architecture.

Raimund Abraham said of his designs: "For me, the piece of paper is the location, and architecture is an intrusion into the location." The design develops from such an elemental operation and formulates a new system of meaning. With this design technique, Abraham also demonstrates a second affinity that is not immediately apparent. In contrast to the tradition of applying meaning to something concrete, he enhances the value of the elemental design process and proceeds without presuppositions from the significant material, thereby using a technique that strongly resembles the central insights of deconstruction. Deconstructivist architecture does not mean that one constructs lines that aren't straight. Rather, it arises when the architect allows architectural significance to proceed from elemental components.

The fact that Raimund Abraham left Austria early in his career certainly left its mark on his work. While associating with the most advanced architects and architectural theorists, he worked out his original convictions about designs that use the great variety of given materials without presuppositions, and he defended his views vehemently. With the Austrian Cultural Forum, he created a setting for the presentation of Austrian culture that is not just a setting, but also—entirely in the sense of contemporary philosophy and cultural theory—generates its own significance. In the powerful surroundings of all the buildings in Midtown Manhattan that are steeped in architectural history, this building is only able to hold its own because of its intellectually compelling nature and its clear concept, and that in turn forces the cultural programming to be highly disciplined and coherent. The building is up-to-date, on the leading edge. By doing without the kitsch of any historical quotations, it blossoms out on its own and enters into a dialogue with its surroundings, programmatically embodying the idea of a cultural forum.

48	Obere Galerie	Upper gallery
49	Lobby	Lobby
50	Nördliche Fassade	North façade
51	Ausstellungsansicht	Exhibition view *NineteenEightyFour*, Nicolas Grospierre & Kobas Laksa, *Series from the Afterlife of Buildings*, 2008, Rachel Owens, *Privet*, 2010, unteres Mezzanin	lower mezzanine; Paul Laffoley, *Physically Alive Structured Environment: The Bauharoque*, 2004, Gerold Tagwerker, *Urban Studies-Toronto*, 2000–2001, obere Galerie	upper gallery

Lebbeus Woods

EIN HERAUSFORDERNDES VERMÄCHTNIS

Es ist bezeichnend, dass Raimund Abraham eines der ehrwürdigsten Prinzipien architektonischer Ordnungen, die Symmetrie, bei seinem Projekt für das Austrian Cultural Forum in New York eingesetzt hat. Anders als die von der École des Beaux-Arts bevorzugte dreiteilige Symmetrie handelt es sich bei Abraham um eine zweiseitige Symmetrie, deren unmittelbarster Bezugspunkt der menschliche Körper ist. Die Symmetrie wurde jedenfalls von den meisten modernen Architekten und Künstlern, die die dynamischere Balance asymmetrischer Konstruktionen vorzogen, verschmäht. Dies stand im Zusammenhang mit den aufkeimenden, sich im Ungleichgewicht befindlichen Formationen der modernen Gesellschaft. Ohne eine Gottheit oder die hierarchische Ordnung einer von Gott bestimmten zentralen Autorität – wie etwa einem Monarchen – musste die moderne, industrielle Gesellschaft ihr Kräftegleichgewicht in einer fortwährend neu verhandelten Anordnung unterschiedlicher und nicht einfach gegensätzlicher, dialektischer Positionen finden. Die Symmetrie jedweder Art ist die Antithese des modernen politischen Prozesses, also der Demokratie, aber auch die Antithese moderner Praktiken in vielen Bereichen, die vor allem mit Wachstum anstelle von Stillstand und kontinuierlicher Veränderung hin zu oftmals nicht genau definierten Zielen zu tun haben. Raimund Abrahams Architektur, wie sie sich im Turm des Austrian Cultural Forum darstellt, hinterfragt diese Begriffe, nicht um voller Nostalgie zu einem vormodernen Staat zurückzukehren, sondern um etwas in ästhetischer und ethischer Hinsicht Neues zu erschaffen.
Um Ahrahams Anspruch und Leistung zu verstehen, ist es notwendig zu wissen, dass er ein Humanist war, der in seinem Diskurs und in seinen Konzepten die Beschaffenheit des Menschen in den Mittelpunkt seines Interesses stellte. Darüber hinaus war er ein Existenzialist, der die persönliche, menschliche Erfahrung jeder Form der Ideologie – sei sie religiös, politisch oder künstlerisch – vorzog. Die Idee der Authentizität, die dem Bewusstsein der Einzigartigkeit jedes Individuums entspringt, stand im Mittelpunkt seiner

Philosophie und bildete somit den Maßstab, nach dem er sich selbst, andere und jedes kreative Schaffen bewertete. Ein architektonisches Werk muss die konsequente Folge der persönlichen Integrität des Architekten sein, seine Wahrhaftigkeit sich selbst gegenüber, und nicht einfach nur ein angenommener Stil oder ein affektiertes Gehabe. Dieses Verlangen nach Authentizität führte dazu, dass er vielen Leuten als zu kritisch erschien, zu moralistisch und in seinen Urteilen zu streng für eine Epoche wie die heutige, die sich durch viele neue Möglichkeiten, eine große Vielfalt und eine Komplexität auszeichnet, die man von einem Standpunkt alleine nicht erfassen und mit nur einem Maßstab nicht messen kann. Allerdings war Abrahams ethische und künstlerische Position weniger rigide, als seine öffentlichen Statements und sein Verhalten manchmal den Anschein erweckten. Die Authentizität liegt in der Individualität begründet, und in letzter Konsequenz verlangte Abraham nur nach einem: nach der authentischen Individualität einer Person und ihrer Werke. Ein Gebäude oder ein Entwurf oder eine Zeichnung oder eine Aussage muss von innen kommen und nicht von Faktoren oder Kräften wie Moden oder politischen Berechnungen, die außerhalb ihrer ursprünglichen Quelle im Individuum liegen, geformt werden. Genau hier, bei seiner Vorstellung vom Ursprünglichen, werden Abrahams Philosophie und ihre Folgen – seine Architektur – höchst komplex.

Jedes Individuum ist einzigartig, ein Ursprung, das ist wahr. Gleichzeitig ist aber die Beschaffenheit des Menschen universal, eine Kondition, die von allen Individuen geteilt wird. Also ist der Ursprung archaisch und nur am Anfang der menschlichen Zeit zu finden. Man könnte sagen, dass die Geschichte die Versuche bezeugt, dieses Paradox zu lösen. Abrahams Auffassung nach lässt sich dieses Paradox nur durch Kreativität lösen, sozusagen durch das Architekturkonzept eines Individuums und durch die Bemühung, das Universelle in Hinblick auf das Persönliche zu formulieren. T. S. Eliots Gedanke: »Wir lassen nie vom Suchen ab, und doch, am Ende all unseren Suchens, sind wir am Ausgangspunkt zurück und werden diesen Ort zum ersten Mal erfassen« findet sich in Abrahams Verlangen nach Originalität wieder, das heißt, vom allgemeinen Ursprung auszugehen und

etwas zum allerersten Mal zu wissen. Wissen ist immer und ausschließlich individuell und persönlich. Wir wissen Dinge und handeln entsprechend unserer Kenntnis, nicht so sehr durch die Interpretation vermittelter, universeller Wahrheiten, sondern vielmehr in Sprüngen inspirierter Vorstellungskraft. Der Turm des Austrian Cultural Forum ist ein solcher Sprung.

Es fällt einem kaum eine anderes Gebäude heutzutage ein, das so deutlich und in einer neuen Synthese sowohl das Archaische als auch das Moderne verkörpert. Abraham selbst hat es anschaulich mit einem »Kopf von der Osterinsel und einer Guillotine« verglichen. Es steht allein in der dichten Städtelandschaft inmitten Manhattans, es hat keine Verwandten oder auch nur verwandte Seelen unter den anderen Türmen. Es ist eine Ikone des Menschlichen, die ein essenzielles, vor langer Zeit vergessenes Geheimnis symbolisiert, während es – so könnte man es sich vorstellen – hinaus auf die Ewigkeit starrt. Seine Hauptfassade ist jedoch ein krasses, zeitgenössisches Konstrukt aus Metall- und Glassegmenten, die darauf warten, auf die Feinde der Revolution hinunterzufallen, also auf die Feinde der letztlich zeitlichen Werte von »Freiheit, Gleichheit, Brüderlichkeit«. Wie ein Kippbild, das uns zwischen zwei sich widersprechenden Bildern und Ideen hin und her schwanken lässt, hinterfragt der Turm die Idee einer Gebäudetypologie an sich. Und wichtiger noch: Er offenbart die paradoxe und schwierige Natur der Originalität.

54

56

52 ACF und Nachbargebäude in Richtung Norden | View of ACF and surrounding buildings facing north
53 6. Stock | 6th floor
54 Wohnung des Direktors | Director's residence
55 Wendeltreppe in der Wohnung des Direktors | Spiral stairway in director's residence
56, 57 Details der Treppenstruktur | Details of stairway structure

57

Lebbeus Woods

A CHALLENGING LEGACY

It is revealing that Raimund Abraham has employed one of the most venerable principles of architectural order—symmetry—in his project for the Austrian Cultural Forum in New York. Unlike the tripartite symmetry favored by the Ecole des Beaux-Arts, his is a bilateral symmetry, related most immediately to the human body. In any event, symmetry was disdained by most modernist architects and artists, who preferred the more dynamic balance of asymmetrical compositions, which had something to do with the off-balance, nascent formations of modern society. Without a godhead, or the hierarchical order of a divinely ordained central authority, such as a monarch, modern industrial society has had to find its balance of forces in a continually negotiated arrangement of diverse and not simply opposing or dialectical positions. Symmetry of any kind is antithetical to modern political processes, which is to say, democracy, but also to modern practices in many fields, which aim above all to be concerned with growth, not stasis, and continual transformation toward often undefined goals. Raimund Abraham's architecture, as exemplified in the Austrian Cultural Forum tower, challenges these notions, not in order to nostalgically return to a premodern state, but rather to create something aesthetically, and ethically, new.

To grasp Abraham's aspiration and achievement, it is necessary to understand that he was a humanist who, in his discourse and concepts, put the human condition at the forefront of his concerns, and an existentialist, who put personal human experience ahead of any form of ideology—religious, political, artistic. The idea of authenticity, which issues from any individual's self-conscious uniqueness, was at the core of his philosophy and thus the standard by which he judged himself, others, and all creative work. A work of architecture must be the consequence of the architect's personal integrity, his trueness to himself, and not merely an adopted style or affectation. This demand for authenticity made him, in many people's eyes, an overly severe critic, far too moralistic and judgmental for an epoch such as the present one, characterized by many new possibilities, diversities, and a complexity that cannot be grasped from any one point of view, or judged by only one standard. However, Abraham's ethical and artistic position was not as rigid as even he sometimes projected by his public pronouncements and

behavior. Authenticity is rooted in individuality, and Abraham was ultimately demanding only that—authentic individuality—of a person and their works. A building, or a design, or a drawing, or an utterance must come from within and not be shaped by factors or forces, such as fashions or political expediencies, external to its source of origin, that is, its originality within the individual. It is precisely here, in his conception of the original, that Abraham's philosophy and its consequence—his architecture—become deeply complex.

Each individual is unique, a point of origin, that is true. Yet at the same time, the human condition is universal, that is, a condition shared by all individuals. Hence, the point of origin is archaic, found only at the beginning of human time. We might say that history is a testament to the attempts to reconcile this paradox. In Abraham's view, the paradox is resolved only creatively, say, in an individual's conception of architecture, and in the struggle to formulate the universal in terms of the personal. T. S. Eliot's thought—"We shall not cease from exploration. And the end of all our exploring will be to arrive where we started and know the place for the first time"—is echoed in Abraham's demand for originality, that is, beginning from the universal point of origin and knowing it for the first time. Knowing is always and only individual and personal. We know, and act on our knowledge, not so much through interpretation of received universal truths but, rather, in leaps of inspired imagination. The Austrian Cultural Forum tower is such a leap.

It is hard to think of another building today that embodies so clearly, and in a new synthesis, both the archaic and the modern. Abraham himself aptly compared it to "an Easter Island head and a guillotine." It stands alone in its crowded mid-Manhattan landscape, without siblings or even kindred spirits among the other towers, an icon of the human symbolizing some essential, long forgotten mystery—staring out, we might imagine, onto eternity. Still, its principal façade is a starkly contemporary construct of metal and glass blades poised to fall on all enemies of the Revolution, enemies, that is, of the ultimately temporal values of "liberty, equality, and fraternity." Like a figure-ground puzzle that has us flipping back and forth between two contradictory images and ideas, the tower challenges the very idea of building typology. More importantly, it is a revelation of the paradoxical and difficult nature of originality.

58   ACF und Nachbargebäude in Richtung Osten | View of ACF and surrounding buildings facing east

59   Blick vom 22. Stock in Richtung Süden | View from the 22nd floor facing south

KENNETH FRAMPTON IM GESPRÄCH MIT ANDRES LEPIK UND ANDREAS STADLER

9. JUNI 2010

ANDRES LEPIK / ANDREAS STADLER: Kann Raimund Abrahams Austrian Cultural Forum zu den vorherrschenden architektonischen Richtungen des späten 20. Jahrhunderts in Bezug gesetzt werden? Ist etwa sein Symbolismus (die Maske, das Rückgrat) in Verbindung mit der Postmoderne zu bringen, oder handelt es sich um ein individuelles Konzept von Abraham?

KENNETH FRAMPTON: Die maskenartige, axiale Form der Arbeiten von Raimund Abraham ist nahezu sein Markenzeichen, aber sie scheint kaum noch in einem Zusammenhang mit dem zu stehen, was man mittlerweile in der Architektur die Postmoderne nennt. Es ist interessant, sich klarzumachen, dass sich diese Form seit 1982 – seit seinem Projekt einer Kirche an der Berliner Mauer – in seinem Werk herausbildet. Eine Reihe ursprünglicher Vorstellungen scheint in dieser Arbeit zusammengekommen zu sein: Da ist zum einen die Abstraktion einer anthropomorphen Figur, die auf unerklärliche Art und Weise in einer Wand gefangen ist, und zum anderen die Andeutung eines Kruzifixes, dargestellt als das Instrument einer rätselhaften Höllenmaschine. Eine Spur davon taucht wieder 1985 in seinem Ca'Venier-Projekt in Venedig sowie in dem 1987 vollendeten Gebäude in der Friedrichstraße in Berlin auf. Eine Version davon findet sich auch in der Straßenfassade des Hypo-Hauses in Lienz (1993–1996), und dann begegnet man ihr beim Austrian Cultural Forum wieder, wo sie sich über die volle Gebäudehöhe erstreckt und dem gesamten Bau eine geheimnisvoll belebte Aura verleiht. Wie auch in Bezug auf andere Aspekte von Raimund Abrahams Arbeiten kommt es auf den Blickwinkel, auf das Wetter, die Tageszeit der Betrachtung und so weiter an. In einem Moment denkt man zum Beispiel, es handele sich beim Austrian Cultural Forum um eine späte konstruktivistische Arbeit, und zu einem anderen Zeitpunkt kann es dann wie eine Art bedrohliche »Anima« wirken, die vielleicht an eine der Figuren von der Osterinsel erinnert oder an eine Stele von Constantin Brâncuși oder an bestimmte Skulpturen von Walter Pichler, die ich vor vielen Jahren in der Londoner Whitechapel Gallery gesehen habe.

AL/AS: Inwieweit ist Abrahams besonderer Ansatz durch Konzepte von Künstlern und Designern wie Walter Pichler oder Friedrich Kiesler inspiriert?

KF: Am Anfang ihrer Karrieren standen Abraham und Pichler miteinander in so enger Verbindung, dass sie sogar ein Bild zusammen zeichnen würden. Was sie verbindet, ist – abgesehen von ihrer Fixierung auf eine latente »Anima« in der Form – vielleicht die Auseinandersetzung mit dem alles verändernden Moment, in dem ein massiver Steinblock auseinanderbricht, oder – was ähnlich unerklärlich ist – mit dem Moment, in dem sich die Erdoberfläche auftut und eine unterirdische Quelle hervorquillt. Vielleicht trifft auch keine meiner Analogien den Punkt. Obwohl Abraham für eine kurze Zeit für Kiesler arbeitete, bin ich der Meinung, dass sie in ihren Empfindsamkeiten kaum weiter voneinander entfernt hätten sein können.

AL/AS: Welche Bedeutung hatte das Austrian Cultural Forum während seiner Planung und Konstruktion für die Architekturszene in New York?

KF: Für mich ist und war das Austrian Cultural Forum das ausdrucksstärkste Gebäude, das seit 1958/59 in Manhattan errichtet wurde. In dieser Zeit wurden das Seagram-Gebäude und das Guggenheim Museum, mit denen man es trotz seiner geringeren Größe in Hinblick auf Intensität und Bestimmtheit durchaus vergleichen kann,

fertiggestellt. Wie jedem, der das Gebäude besucht und sich die Räumlichkeiten anschaut, klar werden sollte, ist das Austrian Cultural Fourm eine 7,6 Meter breite »Bleistiftspitze« – eine Tour de Force, die es zu einer Art verdichtetem Mikrokosmos oder sogar zu einer Miniaturstadt macht. Es bleibt eine Demonstration der Tatsache, dass – wenn eine wahrhaft professionelle Intelligenz am Werk und die Vorstellungskraft stark genug ist – eine Idee trotz aller Platzrestriktionen und programmatischer Überlastung integer zu einem fruchtbaren Ergebnis gebracht werden kann.

60 Nachtansicht | Night view
61 Bibliothek | Library   61

KENNETH FRAMPTON IN CONVERSATION WITH ANDRES LEPIK AND ANDREAS STADLER

JUNE 9, 2010

ANDRES LEPIK / ANDREAS STADLER: Can Raimund Abraham's Austrian Cultural Forum be related to some of the main architectural tendencies of the late twentieth century? For example: Is its symbolism (the mask, the backbone) connected with postmodernism, or is it an individual concept by Abraham?

KENNETH FRAMPTON: This masklike axial form is almost a "signature" in the work of Raimund Abraham, but it barely seems related to what one has come to recognize as the postmodern style in architecture. It is interesting to note how his fixation on this gestalt is something that begins to crystallize in his work with his 1982 project for a church along the Berlin Wall. A number of primordial images seem to come together in this work: on the one hand, the abstraction of an anthropomorphic figure inexplicably trapped in a wall and, on the other, the suggestion of a crucifix seen as the instrument of some enigmatic infernal machine. A trace of this reemerges in the Ca'Venier project for Venice, in 1985, and in the Friedrichstrasse Building, Berlin, completed in 1987. A version of it is also present in the street façade of Hypo House in Lienz (1993–96), and it is there again in Austrian Cultural Forum, where it extends for the full height of the structure and imparts a crypto-animate aura to the entire building. As with other aspects of Raimund's work, it depends on the angle you view it from, along with the weather, the time of day, et cetera. Thus at one moment you might think of the ACF as a late Constructivist work, while at another, it may appear as some kind of ominous anima, reminiscent possibly of an Easter Island figure, or a stelae by Constantin Brâncuşi, or certain sculptures by Walter Pichler which I recall seeing in the Whitechapel Gallery in London many years ago.

AL/AS: How much is Abraham's specific approach inspired by artists' and designers' concepts, such as those of Walter Pichler or Frederick Kiesler?

KF: Early in their careers, Abraham and Pichler were closely associated with each other, even to the extent of sometimes producing an image together. What they share in common perhaps—aside from this obsession with the latent anima in form—is this preoccupation with the cataclysmic moment in which a massive stone block splits apart or, equally inexplicably, a crevice opens up in the earth's surface as a prelude to the outpouring of some subterranean source. Perhaps all these analogies of mine are somewhat wide of the mark. Even though Abraham worked briefly for Kiesler, in my view their sensibilities could hardly be more removed from one another.

AL/AS: What was the relevance of the Austrian Cultural Forum for the architectural scene in New York at the time of its planning and building?

KF: For me, the Austrian Cultural Forum was, and still is, the most powerful piece of architecture to be realized in Manhattan since 1958/59, the years that saw the completion of the Seagram Building and the Guggenheim Museum, to which—in terms of intensity and resolution—it may be surely compared despite its diminutive size. As should be obvious to anyone who visits the building and tours through its facilities, the ACF is a twenty-five-feet-wide "pencil point" tour de force, which

makes it a kind of compressed microcosm or even, at a stretch, a city in miniature. It remains a demonstration of the fact that if a true professional intelligence is present and the vision is strong enough, an idea can be carried through with integrity to a fertile result, despite all the dimensional restrictions and the programmatic congestion.

62 Büro des Direktors | Director's office
63 Blick vom unteren Mezzanin auf die Nordfassade | View of the north façade from the lower mezzanine
64 Dachterrasse | Roof terrace

Peter Marboe

EIN TRAUM WIRD WAHR

Es war einmal … so fangen viele Märchen an. So könnte auch ein Aufsatz über den Neubau des – damals noch Österreichisches Kulturinstitut genannten – Austrian Cultural Forum in New York beginnen. Es war also einmal ein junger, österreichischer Architekt, Raimund Abraham, der kam nach New York, lernte dort berühmte Kollegen kennen, wurde von Friedrich Kiesler gefördert und entwickelte sehr bald seine eigenen Visionen einer ganz neuen, radikalen, zukunftsweisenden Architektur. Er schrieb darüber, entwarf Projekte, baute das eine oder andere und unterrichtete an berühmten Architekturzentren. Aber für die Realisierung seiner wirklich großen, das städtische Erscheinungsbild verändernden Vorhaben wollte sich kein geeigneter Bauherr finden lassen. Und dann geschah das kleine Wunder – aber auch Wunder haben ihre Vorgeschichte …

Das alte Kulturinstitut, ein liebenswertes, fast neunzig Jahre altes Sandsteingebäude bedurfte einer sehr aufwendigen Generalsanierung, die weder neuen Raum noch neue Architektur hätte schaffen können. Was vielen kühn schien, war eigentlich nur folgerichtig, nämlich an das Außenministerium in Wien zu berichten, dass stattdessen ein Neubau ins Auge gefasst werden sollte. Dieser würde – nach Schätzung des verdienten Vertrauensarchitekten Gerhard E. Karplus rund dreimal so teuer – zwei enorme Vorteile bieten: mehr Raum und, vor allem, in New York, einem der großen Weltkulturzentren, ein nachhaltiges Statement zeitgenössischer, österreichischer Architektur. Im Frühjahr 1987 – Zufall oder Fügung (bei einem Märchen weiß man das nie so genau) – konnte der damalige Außenminister Alois Mock anlässlich eines Besuches in New York mit diesem Vorschlag vertraut gemacht werden.

»Nichts Edles ist jemals ohne Leidenschaft geschaffen worden«, heißt es bei Ferdinand Raimund. Alois Mock entwickelte von Beginn an jene Leidenschaft für dieses Projekt, die Voraussetzung dafür war, dass seitens des Außenministeriums Neuland beschritten, Einwände (vor allem wirtschaftlicher Natur) entkräftet, Widerstände beseitigt und die komplexen, organisatorischen Probleme dieses bis dahin größten, öffentlichen Wettbewerbs (458 Abholungen, 226 Teilnehmer) bewältigt werden konnten. Allen Versuchen, dieses Unterfangen, mit dem österreichische Architekturgeschichte in

65 ACF und 52. Straße in Richtung Osten | View of ACF and 52nd Street facing east

66 Ausstellungsansicht | Exhibition view *Creative Migration*, Johannes Girardoni & Astrid Steiner, *7 Minutes 20 Seconds*, 2009, Hauptgalerie | main gallery

New York geschrieben werden sollte, im Rahmen eines kleinen, begrenzten Einladungswettbewerbs abzuwickeln, widersetzte er sich konsequent. Zur Ehre der »Großen«, die das gern gesehen hätten, sei gesagt, dass sie sich nach anfänglichem Zögern doch zur Teilnahme bereit erklärt haben.

Der Schlüssel zur erfolgreichen Durchführung eines solchen Wettbewerbs ist die Jury. Von ihrer Kompetenz und Integrität hängen Akzeptanz und Durchführbarkeit ab. Die drei Tage im damaligen Messepalast mit den 226 aufgestellten Objekten und den oft sehr emotionalen, argumentativen und nach allen Richtungen offenen Diskussionen, vor allem natürlich, als es um die Runde der letzten drei Projekte ging, werden unvergesslich bleiben. Unvergesslich ist auch der Moment, als nach dem strikt anonym abgewickelten Wettbewerb das Kuvert des Erstgereihten mit der Nummer 49 geöffnet wurde: Raimund Abraham. Auch wenn es kitschig klingen mag, aber ein Traum, an den er fest geglaubt hatte, wie er mir im ersten Telefonat versicherte, war für ihn wahr geworden. Ein Traum, der durch die Verpflichtung des Außenministeriums zur Baubeauftragung an den Erstgereihten auch in Erfüllung gehen würde und dessen Integrität durch eine Jury, »der sich auch die Großen beugen mussten«, wie die Zeitungen damals schrieben, sichergestellt war.

Das weltweite, mediale Echo in praktisch allen wichtigen Tages- und Wochenzeitungen, Magazinen und Fachzeitschriften trug sicher auch wesentlich dazu bei, dass dieses außergewöhnliche Projekt auf breiter Basis akzeptiert wurde. Nach einer echten »Schrecksekunde« – der junge Kurzzeit-Finanzminister Andreas Staribacher hatte überraschend die geplante Sonderfinanzierung aus dem Budget verweigert – fand Mocks Nachfolger Wolfgang Schüssel einen außerbudgetären Finanzierungsmodus, der im Parlament einstimmig, also von allen politischen Parteien, beschlossen wurde.

Raimund Abraham wollte aber die radikale Kühnheit seiner Architektur auch als Einladung verstanden wissen, »mutig in die neuen Zeiten zu schreiten« (wie es auch in der österreichischen Bundeshymne heißt). Innen- und Außenleben, Programm und äußeres Erscheinungsbild des Kulturforums sollten miteinander im Einklang stehen, die neuen Räume Plattform eines lebendigen, zeitgenössischen, künstlerischen Diskurses sein.

Für die Republik Österreich war dieses außergewöhnliche Bauprojekt eine Abenteuerreise, die untrennbar mit den Namen Mock, Waldner, Thun-Hohenstein, Son, Bliem, Niesner, Preissl, den Mitgliedern der Jury, und einigen anderen verbunden bleibt. Für Raimund Abraham, den – unabhängig von formalen Staatsbürgerschaften – Patrioten und Weltbürger in einem, war es ein Triumph visionärer Kreativität und künstlerischer Konsequenz. Seine Botschaft wird noch lange von allen, die diesem großen Architekten in »seinem« Austrian Cultural Forum begegnen werden, gehört und – hoffentlich – verstanden werden.

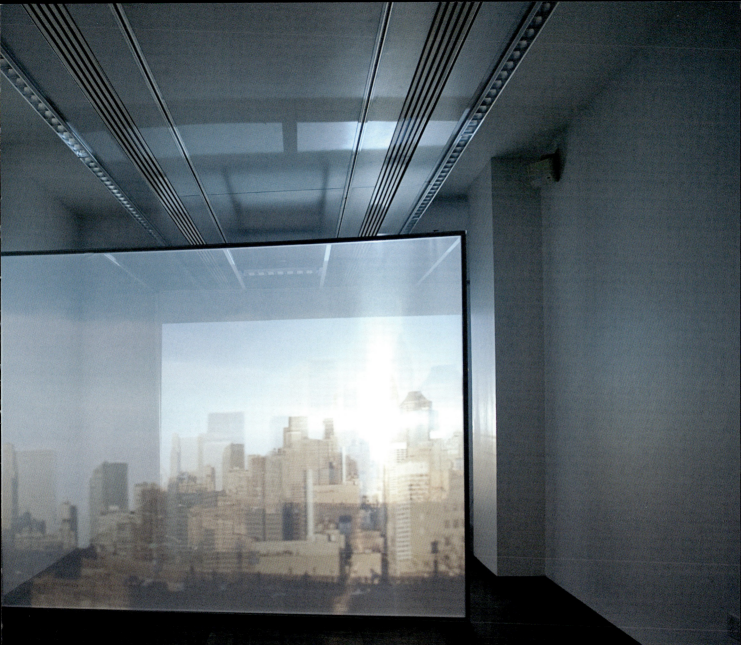

Peter Marboe

A DREAM COME TRUE

Once upon a time . . . That's how many fairy tales begin. It's also how an essay about the new building for the Austrian Cultural Forum in New York could begin—back then it was still called the Austrian Cultural Institute. So let's begin. Once upon a time there was a young Austrian architect called Raimund Abraham who travelled to New York, got to know some famous colleagues there, had his work promoted by Frederick Kiesler, and soon developed his own vision of an entirely new and radical architecture of the future. He wrote articles about it, designed projects, built one or two of them, and taught at renowned centers for architecture. But he couldn't realize his really great plans, the plans that would change the appearance of the city, because no one was willing to commission him to build such a building. And then there was a miracle—but even a miracle has a background story . . .

The old Cultural Institute, a charming sandstone building that was almost ninety years old, was in need of very extensive renovations, but even if the renovations had been undertaken, they could not have created new space or new architecture. So what seemed bold to many was actually the only logical thing to do. A report was sent to the Foreign Ministry suggesting that they consider a brand-new building instead. Even though the trusted and respected architect Gerhard E. Karplus estimated it would cost roughly three times as much, there would be two tremendous advantages to a new building: more space and, most importantly, a lasting statement of contemporary Austrian architecture in New York, one of the great cultural centers of the world. In the spring of 1987—by coincidence or the hand of fate (in a fairy tale, you're never quite sure which)—we were able to inform the Foreign Minister, Alois Mock, of our plan when he was visiting New York.

In the words of Ferdinand Raimund, "Nothing magnificent has ever been created without passion." From the beginning, Alois Mock had the necessary passion for this project to ensure that the Foreign Ministry broke new ground. Objections (mainly of an economic nature) were refuted, opposition was mollified, and the complex problems of organizing this open competition—the largest yet (458 expressions of interest, 226 submitted projects)—could be dealt with. With this undertaking, Austrian architectural

history would be written in New York, and Mock consistently opposed all attempts to turn it into a smaller, invitational competition. To the credit of the "big names" that would have preferred that it be invitational, it must be said that they overcame their initial hesitation and agreed to participate anyway.

The key to carrying out such a competition successfully is the jury. Their competence and integrity determine the workability of the competition and the acceptance of the results. None of us will ever forget the three days in what was then the Exhibition Palace, where the 226 models were set up. The discussions were often very emotional, argumentative, and open in all directions, particularly when we had it narrowed down to the last three contestants. The competition was kept strictly anonymous. It was an unforgettable moment when the envelope of the project we had ranked first, project number 49, was opened, identifying the winner: Raimund Abraham. It may sound strange, but when I first spoke with him on the phone, he told me he had already had a dream about it, a dream he firmly believed in, and now the dream had come true. It was a dream that would be fulfilled thanks to the commitment of the Foreign Ministry to commission the winner to construct the building, and because its integrity was guaranteed by a jury "to whom even the big names must bow," as the newspapers put it.

The worldwide echo in the media—in practically all the important daily and weekly papers, magazines, and architectural journals—was certainly instrumental in having this remarkable project so broadly accepted. After a genuine "moment of shock"—the young, short-term Minister of Finance, Andreas Staribacher, had surprisingly refused the planned special financing from the Ministry's budget—Mock's successor, Wolfgang Schüssel, found an extrabudgetary means of financing the project that was unanimously approved in the Austrian Parliament, by all political parties.

Raimund Abraham wanted people to understand the radical boldness of his architecture as an invitation "to stride with courage into a new age" (to quote the Austrian national anthem). "Inner and Outer Life"—the program and the external appearance of the Cultural Forum were to be in accord with one another, and the new rooms were to be the platform for lively, contemporary, artistic discourse.

For the Republic of Austria, this remarkable construction project was an adventurous voyage that will remain inseparably associated with the names Mock, Waldner, Thun-Hohenstein, Son, Bliem, Niesner, Preissl, the members of the jury, and others. For Raimund Abraham, patriot and world citizen in one—regardless of his formal citizenship—it was a triumph of visionary creativity and artistic consistency. His message will still be heard and, hopefully, understood for a long time by all who encounter this great architect in "his" Austrian Cultural Forum.

67 Detail der Fassade | Detail of façade
68 Hauptgalerie | Main gallery
69 Raimund Abraham, 2002, Fassade | façade

BIOGRAFIEN

RAIMUND ABRAHAM, geboren 1933 in Lienz, Osttirol, war Architekt, Künstler, Theoretiker und Lehrer. Er studierte Architektur an der Technischen Universität Graz. Nach kurzer Tätigkeit als Architekt in Österreich übernahm er 1964 eine Professur an der Rhode Island School of Design in Providence und siedelte in die Vereinigten Staaten über. 1971 wechselte er an die Cooper Union School of Architecture, New York, und wurde zugleich Professor am Pratt Institute. 1992 gewann Abraham den ersten Preis im Wettbewerb für den Neubau des Österreichischen Kulturinstituts in New York. Diesem Bauwerk, das zum wichtigsten seiner Karriere wurde, widmete Abraham zehn Jahre seines Lebens. 2003 wurde er Fakultätsmitglied am Southern California Institute of Architecture (SCI-Arc). Abraham, der die letzten Jahre in New York und in Mazunte, Mexiko, lebte, starb am 4. März 2010 in Los Angeles.

PETER ENGELMANN, geboren 1947 in Berlin, ist Philosoph und Verleger. Er studierte Philosophie und Soziologie in Berlin, Paris und Bremen und promovierte über Hegel. 1985 gründete Engelmann in Wien die Edition Passagen, 1987 den Passagen Verlag. Er ist Herausgeber vieler Autoren der Postmoderne und Dekonstruktion. Engelmann lehrte Philosophie an Universitäten in Deutschland, Österreich und den USA und ist Autor zahlreicher Texte zur Philosophie.

KENNETH FRAMPTON, geboren 1930 in Woking, Surrey, studierte Architektur an der Architectural Association in London. Er lehrte an einer Reihe führender Institutionen wie dem Royal College of Art in London, der ETH Zürich, der EPFL Lausanne, der Accademia di Architettura in Mendrisio und dem Berlage Institute in den Niederlanden.

ANDRES LEPIK, geboren 1961 in Augsburg, ist Architekturhistoriker und Kurator. Er studierte Kunstgeschichte in Augsburg und München und promovierte 1990. Von 1994 bis 2007 war er Kurator an der Nationalgalerie und Leiter der Architekturabteilung 20./21. Jahrhundert an der Kunstbibliothek der Staatlichen Museen zu Berlin. Seit 2007 ist er Kurator für zeitgenössische Architektur am Museum of Modern Art, New York.

PETER MARBOE, geboren 1942 in Wien, ist Politiker (ÖVP) und Intendant. Er studierte Jura in Wien und promovierte 1965. Ab 1967 arbeitete er in der Kulturabteilung des Bundespressedienstes, 1969 wurde er Sekretär von Bundeskanzler Josef Klaus. Von 1970 an arbeite er in verschiedenen Funktionen in den USA. Von 1991 bis 1996 war er Leiter der Kulturpolitischen Sektion im Außenministerium, von 1996 bis 2001 Stadtrat für Kultur in Wien und von 2003 bis 2007 Intendant des Wiener Mozartjahres 2006.

GERALD MATT, geboren 1958 in Hard / Bregenz, Vorarlberg, studierte Rechtswissenschaften, Kunstgeschichte und Betriebswirtschaft und ist seit 1996 Direktor der Kunsthalle Wien. Matt hat zahlreiche Ausstellungen kuratiert und Publikationen zu zeitgenössischer Kunst und Kulturmanagement herausgegeben. Er ist Gastprofessor an der Universität für angewandte Kunst in Wien und Dozent an der CIAM Hochschule in Köln.

ANDREAS STADLER, geboren 1965 in Mürzzuschlag, Steiermark, ist Diplomat. Er studierte Politikwissenschaften in Wien, Warschau und Florenz. Er war stellvertretender Botschafter Österreichs in Zagreb, Direktor des Österreichischen Kulturforums in Warschau und Berater für Wissenschaft, Kunst und Kultur beim Österreichischen Bundespräsidenten. Seit 2007 ist er Direktor des Austrian Cultural Forum New York. Auch publiziert er in den Bereichen Internationale Beziehungen und Kulturpolitik.

LEBBEUS WOODS, geboren 1940 in Lansing, Michigan, ist Architekt, Lehrer und Kritiker. Seine Schwerpunkte sind experimentelle Projekte und die kritische Transformation von Gebäuden, Städten und Landschaften. Woods lehrt an der European Graduate School in Saas-Fee und ist Architekturprofessor an der Cooper Union School of Architecture, New York.

BIOGRAPHIES

RAIMUND ABRAHAM, born 1933 in Lienz, East Tirol, was an architect, artist, theoretician, and teacher. After studying architecture at Graz University of Technology, he worked for a brief time as an architect in Austria. In 1964 he was offered a professorship at the Rhode Island School of Design in Providence and relocated to the United States. In 1971 Abraham switched to The Cooper Union School of Architecture in New York City, while at the same time becoming a professor at Pratt Institute. In 1992 he won first prize in the architectural design competition for the new Austrian Cultural Institute building in New York. Abraham devoted ten years of his life to this building, the most important of his career. In 2003 he became a member of the faculty at the Southern California Institute of Architecture (SCI-Arc). Abraham spent the last years of his life in New York and Mazunte, Mexico, and died on March 4, 2010 in Los Angeles.

PETER ENGELMANN, born 1947 in Berlin, is a philosopher and publisher. He studied philosophy and sociology in Berlin, Paris, and Bremen, earning his doctorate on the topic of Hegel. In 1985 Engelmann founded Edition Passagen in Vienna, and in 1987 the Passagen Verlag, where he publishes many postmodernist and deconstructivist authors. Engelmann teaches philosophy at universities in Germany, Austria, and the United States and has authored many works on the subject.

KENNETH FRAMPTON, born 1930 in Woking, Surrey, trained as an architect at the Architectural Association School of Architecture, London. He has taught at a number of leading institutions, including the Royal College of Art in London, the ETH Zurich, the EPFL Lausanne, the Accademia di Architettura in Mendrisio, and the Berlage Institute in Rotterdam.

ANDRES LEPIK, born 1961 in Augsburg, is an architectural historian and curator. He studied art history in Augsburg and Munich and earned his doctorate in 1990. From 1994 to 2007 he was a curator at the National Gallery and director of the Department of 20th and 21st Century Architecture at the Art Library of the National Museums in Berlin. Since 2007 he has been the curator for contemporary architecture at The Museum of Modern Art in New York.

PETER MARBOE, born 1942 in Vienna, is a politician (Austrian People's Party [ÖVP]) and artistic director. He studied law in Vienna and earned his doctorate in 1965. Beginning in 1967 he went to work for the Cultural Department of the Federal Press Service, and in 1969 he became the secretary of Federal Chancellor Josef Klaus. Beginning in 1970, he worked in various capacities in the USA. From 1991 to 1996 he was the General Director of the Cultural Policy Section in the Foreign Ministry and from 1996 to 2001 the Executive Councillor for culture in Vienna. From 2003 to 2007 he served as artistic director of the Vienna Mozart Year 2006.

GERALD MATT, born 1958 in Hard/Bregenz, Vorarlberg, studied law, art history, and business administration. He has been directing the Kunsthalle in Vienna since 1996. Matt has curated numerous exhibitions and edited various publications about contemporary art and cultural management. Matt is a guest professor at the University for Applied Arts in Vienna and lectures at the Center for International Arts Management (CIAM) at the Cologne University of Music and Dance.

ANDREAS STADLER, born 1965 in Mürzzuschlag, Styria, is a diplomat who studied political science in Vienna, Warsaw, and Florence. Stadler was Deputy Ambassador of Austria in Zagreb, director of the Austrian Cultural Forum in Warsaw, and advisor for science, art, and culture to the Austrian Federal President. He has been the director of the Austrian Cultural Forum New York since 2007 and publishes on international relations and cultural politics.

LEBBEUS WOODS, born 1940 in Lansing, Michigan, is an architect, teacher, and critic whose work focuses on experimentation and the critical transformations of buildings, cities, and landscapes. He is on the faculty of The European Graduate School in Saas-Fee, Switzerland and is professor of architecture at The Cooper Union School of Architecture in New York.

BIBLIOGRAFIE (AUSWAHL)
BIBLIOGRAPHY (SELECTION)

Raimund Abraham, *Elementare Architektur*, mit Fotografien von | with photographs by Josef Dapra, Salzburg 1963.

Architekturzentrum Wien (Hrsg. | ed.), *Manhattan Austria. Die Architektur des österreichischen Kulturinstitutes von Raimund Abraham | The Architecture of the Austrian Cultural Institute by Raimund Abraham*, Ausst.-Kat. | exh. cat. Architekturzentrum Wien, Wien | Vienna 1999.

Ernst Bliem (Hrsg. | ed.), *Österreichische Architektur in N.Y. Ein baukünstlerischer Wettbewerb | An Architectural Competition*, Innsbruck 1993.

Brigitte Groihofer (Hrsg. | ed.), *Raimund Abraham. [Un]built*, Wien und New York | Vienna and New York 1996.

Ada Louise Huxtable, »Merging Culture and Commerce in Architecture«, in: *The Wall Street Journal*, 16.5.2002.

Julie V. Iovine, »For Austria. A Tribute and Protest«, in: *The New York Times*, 7.3.2002.

Herbert Muschamp, »A Gift of Vienna that Skips the Schlag«, in: *The New York Times*, 19.4.2002.

Walter Seidl, *Zwischen Kultur und Culture. Das Austrian Institute in New York und Österreichs kulturelle Repräsentanz in den USA*, Wien | Vienna 2001.

Christoph Thun-Hohenstein (Hrsg. | ed.), *Celebrating Five Years at the Forum*, New York 2007.

Editors of Wallpaper Magazine (Hrsg. | ed.), *Wallpaper City Guide New York*, London 2009.

Wiener Zeitung (Hrsg. | ed.), »Das Österreichische Kulturforum New York«, Verlagsbeilage | insert, 1.5.2009.

ABBILDUNGSNACHWEIS
IMAGE CREDITS

Cover, S. | p. 123: Dodo Jin Ming: Courtesy of the Brooklyn Rail; S. | pp. 6/7, 8/9, 10/11, 14/15, 17, 19, 26/27, 28/29, 31, 32/33, 36/37, 39, 41, 42/43, 65, 69, 70/71, 76/77, 80/81, 89, 98/99, 102/103, 115, 116/117, 119, 120/121, Rückseite | back cover: David Plakke/davidplakke.com; S. | pp. 12/13, 22/23, 24/25, 67, 73, 75, 79, 83, 85, 87, 91, 92/93, 94/95, 96/97, 101, 105, 106/107, 109, 110/111, 112/113: Robert Polidori; S. | pp. 25/26: Lucinda Devlin: Courtesy of Galerie m Bochum, Bochum; S. | p. 26 oben | top: Mathilde ter Heijne: Courtesy of La Collezione Le Gaia, Italia; S. | p. 26 unten | bottom: Steven Cohen: Courtesy of the artist, © Marianne Greber; S. | p. 28 oben | top: Anja Hitzenberger: Courtesy of the artist; S. | pp. 28/29: Serge Spitzer: Courtesy of the artist and Foundation 2021; Thomas Feuerstein: Courtesy of the artist; S. | pp. 31–33: Judith Fegerl: Courtesy of the artist; S. | p. 35: Sylvia Gardner-Wittgenstein; S. | pp. 36/37: Balam Bartolomé: Courtesy of the artist; S. | p. 41: Marlene Haring: Courtesy of the artist; S. | pp. 42/43: Ayad Alkhadi: Courtesy of the artist and ArtSpace Gallery, Dubai; Sarah Rahbar: Courtesy of the artist; S. | pp. 44/45: Daphne Youree; S. | p. 46: Andrew Alberts; S. | pp. 47–63: Pläne | Drawings: Die Republik Österreich | The Republic of Austria; S. | p. 89: Nicolas Grospierre & Kobas Laksa: Courtesy of the artists and Zacheta National Gallery of Art, Warsaw; Rachel Owens: Courtesy of the artist and ZieherSmith Gallery; Gerold Tagwerker: Courtesy of Galerie Grita Insam, Vienna; Paul Laffoley: Courtesy of the artist and Kent Gallery, New York; S. | p. 116: Johannes Girardoni & Astrid Steiner: Courtesy of the artists; S. | p. 124: Matthias Cremer

HERAUSGEBER | EDITORS:
Andres Lepik, Andreas Stadler
REDAKTION | EDITING: Maria Simma
VERLAGSLEKTORAT | COPYEDITING:
Dawn Michelle d'Atri, Julika Zimmermann
ÜBERSETZUNGEN | TRANSLATIONS:
Sibylle Luig, Jean M. Snook, Geoffrey Steinherz
GRAFISCHE GESTALTUNG | GRAPHIC DESIGN:
Verena Gerlach
SCHRIFT | TYPEFACE: Zurich BT
VERLAGSHERSTELLUNG | PRODUCTION:
Stefanie Langner
REPRODUKTIONEN | REPRODUCTIONS:
LVD Gesellschaft für Datenverarbeitung mbH
DRUCK | PRINTING:
Dr. Cantz'sche Druckerei, Ostfildern
PAPIER | PAPER: EuroBulk, 150 g/m²
BUCHBINDEREI | BINDING: Conzella Verlagsbuchbinderei, Urban Meister GmbH, Aschheim-Dornach

© 2010 Hatje Cantz Verlag, Ostfildern; und Autoren | and authors

Erschienen im | Published by
Hatje Cantz Verlag
Zeppelinstrasse 32
73760 Ostfildern
Deutschland | Germany
Tel. +49 711 4405-200
Fax +49 711 4405-220
www.hatjecantz.com

Hatje Cantz books are available internationally at selected bookstores. For more information about our distribution partners, please visit our homepage at www.hatjecantz.com.

ISBN 978-3-7757-2725-9
Printed in Germany

UMSCHLAGABBILDUNGEN
COVER ILLUSTRATIONS:
Vorne | Front: Raimund Abraham, 2002, Fassade | Façade, Foto | photo: Dodo Jin Ming, Courtesy of the Brooklyn Rail
Hinten | back: ACF in Richtung Norden | view of ACF facing north, Foto | photo: David Plakke/davidplakke.com

Austrian Cultural Forum New York
11 East 52nd Street, New York, NY 10022, USA
Tel. +1 212 319-5300, Fax +1 212 644-8660
www.acfny.org